roses

roses

selecting · growing · maintaining

ANDREW MIKOLAJSKI

Consultant Lin Hawthorne

This edition published in the UK in 2007 by
Apple Press
Sheridan House
114 Western Road
Hove
East Sussex BN3 1DD
www.apple-press.com

ISBN: 978 1 84543 208 9

This book was designed and produced by
Anness Publishing Ltd
Hermes House
88–89 Blackfriars Road
London SE1 8HA
www.annesspublishing.com

Contents

Introduction

Highly prized for centuries, the rose is justly called the Queen of Flowers. It is probably true to say that for as long as people have made gardens, they have grown roses in them. Indeed, it would be impossible to exaggerate the rose's importance as the *nonpareil* among garden plants, and its mystique transcends the usual cultural barriers. The rose is the quintessential flower of summer, and with its myriad hues, scents and shapes, it is the perfect companion to many plants in the garden. Once established, the rose will continue to give pleasure for many years.

■ RIGHT
'Pink Bells', one of the larger ground-cover roses, has a spread of about 1.2m/4ft, but it is a real eye-catcher where there is space for it.

Introduction

The long history of rose breeding means that today we enjoy an enormous variety of lovely plants. Apart from the beauty of the flowers, many modern varieties have a long flowering season and good disease resistance. There are forms and styles suitable for nearly every situation, from diminutive patio bushes to huge ramblers cascading from pergolas. The range of colours has never been wider, either, from delicate pastels to vibrant reds, yellows and oranges.

 LEFT
The award-winning 'Top Marks', with its radiant orange-red flowers, is a classic example of a dwarf cluster-flowered or patio rose.

■ **BELOW**
One of the best of the yellow roses, the cluster-flowered (floribunda) 'Arthur Bell' shines out against a backdrop of clipped yew.

We have come to expect a great deal from roses, and with thoughtful choice and careful cultivation they reward us with glorious flowers from spring until the dark days of winter; with scent that fills the summer garden and lingers on in oils, preserves and pot-pourri; and with decorative hips, leaves and even thorns.

The genus *Rosa* actually includes some 150 species of evergreen and deciduous shrubs and climbers as well as many

■ RIGHT
'White Pet', one of the first miniature
roses, has stood the test of time.

■ RIGHT
'White Pet', one of the first miniature
roses, has stood the test of time.

thousands of hybrid cultivars,
which have been developed
from the species over the
centuries. The rose has been
known in cultivation since
humankind first gardened, so
we should not be surprised that
there are roses to suit almost
every climate and situation.

Roses occur naturally in a
wide range of habitats. In the
wild, the majority of roses
bloom only once, usually in
one glorious and frequently
spectacular summer flush,
followed by the hips or fruits
that guarantee the next
generation. Over the centuries,
however, rose breeders have
succeeded in creating not only
plants that produce more and
better flowers but also many
willing, hard-working shrubs
that display their flowers
repeatedly or continuously over
very many months – a feature
that cannot be equalled by any
other single group of shrubs.
Roses now vary in size from
the smallest miniatures, no more
than 25cm/10in in height, to
scrambling ramblers,

which may achieve 30m/100ft
if left to their own devices.
Almost without exception they
are valued for their beautiful,
often richly fragrant blooms,
but many also have foliage that
is attractive in its own right as
well as providing an admirable
foil for the flowers.

Roses offer an extraordinary
diversity of habit: there are
upright or arching shrubs;
dense, thicket-forming bushes;
and trailing and scrambling
ramblers and climbers.

While not everyone would
aspire to a country cottage with
roses scrambling around the
front door, the diversity of rose
form and habit means that
there is a rose to suit every
garden, traditional or ultra-
modern, from the largest plot
to the smallest balcony. Some
of these choices are described
on the pages that follow, with
advice on the care of your roses
to ensure that they continue to
reward you with colour and
scent for years to come.

A History of the Rose

*F*or centuries the rose has been a significant symbol, often adopted by royalty as an emblem. It is a well-known flower, recognized by gardeners and non-gardeners alike. Probably a native of the northern hemisphere, roses have been carried by settlers all over the world, where they have adapted and flourished. Now the world's most beloved flower, this remarkably varied species has a rich and colourful history.

■ RIGHT
The soft pink flowers of the gallica rose 'Duchesse de Montebello' are well loved for their sweet scent.

A history of the rose

Prized, cherished and fought over for centuries, roses now grow all over the world, although they are almost certainly indigenous to the northern hemisphere. Rose fossils, millions of years old, have been found only north of the equator, suggesting that those species now growing in South Africa, South America and Australia were taken there by immigrants.

Roses in ancient times

The wild rose was most certainly enjoyed by early people for its sweet petals and tasty hips, and rose cultivation probably began around 5,000 years ago in China and Persia (modern Iran). In antiquity the rose was regarded as the sacred flower of Venus, and Herodotus, writing about 430 BC, mentioned 60-petalled roses in the gardens of King Midas. In the *Iliad*, Homer's epic composed around 700 BC, the poet tells how Achilles' shield was decorated with roses to celebrate his victory over Hector and that the goddess Aphrodite anointed Hector's body

■ RIGHT
One of the best known and most ancient of all historic roses, *Rosa gallica* var. *officinalis*, was widely grown for its scent in the Middle Ages.

with "ambrosial oil of roses" before it was embalmed.

The roses mentioned by the Greek historians were almost certainly *Rosa gallica*, the ancestor of numerous European roses and so named by Linnaeus in 1753. *R. gallica* var. *officinalis* (syn. *R. officinalis*), which is also known as the apothecary's rose, the crimson damask rose, the red rose of Lancaster and Provins rose, was the main source of rose oil and medicinal preparations in Europe until roses from the Far East were introduced.

The early Christian church condemned roses as a symbol of depravity, and with some reason, since Nero's obsession with the

flowers is widely believed to have contributed to the fall of the Roman Empire. The emperor's excesses were notorious, and it is said that tonnes of roses were required for the numerous banquets he gave. Vast quantities of petals were showered over people at orgies – it is said that at least one participant suffocated – and baths filled with pure rose water were offered to all the guests.

Roses symbolized success in Roman times, and consequently peasants came to believe that it was more profitable to grow roses than corn, a disastrous misconception that was noted by the poet Horace and other contemporary writers.

■ BELOW
Adopted by the House of York as its emblem in 15th-century England, *Rosa* × *alba* is still grown in gardens today. This is *R.* × *alba* 'Alba Semiplena', a semi-double variety grown in some parts of the world for the production of the essential oil, attar.

The Middle Ages

Little information exists about the cultivation of roses in Europe until about AD 400, when the Church adopted the white *R.* × *alba* as the emblem of the Virgin Mary, who is called the "rose without thorns". St Ambrose, who died in AD 397, recounted the legend that the rose grew without thorns until the Fall of Man.

In 1272, on his return from the eighth Crusade, Edward of England (later Edward I), ordered that rose trees should be planted in the gardens surrounding the Tower of London, and he chose a golden rose as his own symbol.

It is possible that the returning crusaders were responsible for the introduction to Europe of *R.* × *damascena* (the damask rose). By the end of the 15th century *R.* × *damascena* var. *semperflorens* (syn. *R.* × *damascena* var. *bifera*) was growing in English gardens. This rose, known as the autumn damask rose, the rose of Castille, the rose of Paestum and, from its French name "Quatre Saisons", the four seasons rose, was the first grown in Europe to produce two crops of flowers every summer.

It is debatable if *R. gallica* was brought to England by the Romans

or at a later date by the returning crusaders, but the red *R. gallica* var. *officinalis* was chosen as the emblem of the House of Lancaster in the prolonged struggle against the House of York (which adopted *R.* × *alba*) during the bitter Wars of the Roses in the 15th century.

The marriage of Henry Tudor (later Henry VII) and Elizabeth of York in 1486 finally united the factions. Their emblem was a white rose in the centre of a red rose entwined with a crown. Since that time the British royal family has adopted the rose as its own.

By the end of the 16th century *R. foetida*, known as the Austrian briar or Austrian yellow rose, had been introduced into Europe from

Persia (now Iran), and *R. moschata*, the musk rose, was certainly favoured by the court of Henry VIII.

European roses were taken to the New World by the Pilgrim Fathers, the dissenters who fled religious persecution in Europe in 1620, and by the mid-17th century they were being grown in many gardens in Massachusetts. North America already had its own species, *R. virginiana* (syn. *R. lucida*) and *R. carolina*. Another species, *R. setigera*, the prairie rose, was later to produce some vigorous rambler cultivars, including the pale pink 'Baltimore Belle', which is still famous in the United States, and the climber 'Long John Silver', which bears fragrant, pure white flowers.

Rosa × odorata 'Pallida', the old blush China rose, is one of the original China roses and was one of the most important introductions, bringing repeat-flowering genes to the modern rose. Its scent and long flowering season ensure that it is still planted by rose lovers.

Early hybrids

Until the process of hybridization was completely understood in the 19th century, new rose varieties were the results of natural crosses or sports (mutations), which were carefully chosen and nurtured by gardeners and nurserymen.

Dutch breeders pioneered work in Europe in the 17th century, working on *R. × centifolia*, which was called the cabbage rose because of the 'hundred-leaved' flowers. Moss roses first appeared around the mid-18th century as a sport from *R. × centifolia*. Rose breeding was also given tremendous impetus by the patronage of the Empress Josephine, the wife of Napoleon Bonaparte. Between 1803 and 1814 she commissioned botanists and nurserymen from all over the world to discover and breed new roses for her garden at Malmaison near Paris, where she eventually grew more than 250 varieties.

■ ABOVE
Introduced in 1932, 'The Fairy' is one of the oldest ground-cover roses. It is usually a healthy plant, with blooms from late summer to early autumn.

Far East introductions

The Chinese had been growing roses for thousands of years before they began to reach European growers in the late 18th century. Around 1781 a pink rose, sometimes known as the old blush China rose (now thought to be *R. × odorata* 'Pallida'), was planted in the Netherlands and was soon taken to Britain. In 1792 a captain of the British East India Company returned home with a red form of the same rose, which he had found growing in Calcutta, and it was named *R. semperflorens* or 'Slater's Crimson China'. Between them, these two roses are responsible for the remontant or repeat-flowering qualities in most modern roses.

At the beginning of the 19th century the flowers known as tea roses arrived on the ships of the British East India Company – their main cargo was tea, which probably accounts for the common name of these roses. They became fashionable in Europe, but because many of them are tender the Victorians grew them in grand conservatories, along with other exotic flowers brought back by explorers and botanists from all parts of the British empire.

■ BELOW
'Souvenir de la Malmaison', first introduced in 1843, bears beautiful and strongly scented flowers in soft powder pink. There are also climbing and bush forms of this famous old Bourbon rose.

East meets West

One of the first marriages between a rose from the West and one from the East was probably a cross between *R. × damascena* var. *semperflorens*, the autumn damask, and a red China rose, which was probably obtained from France by the 2nd Duchess of Portland, an enthusiastic rose collector of the late 18th century. The Portland roses, as they came to be known, were very popular in the early 1800s. Although few survive today, they are ideal for growing in containers and are prized for their perfume and ability to flower throughout the summer.

Meanwhile, at around the same time in Charleston, South Carolina, a rice-grower called John Champney crossed a musk rose, *R. moschata*, with a China rose, 'Parson's Pink' (now known as *R. × odorata* 'Pallida'), which had been a gift from his friend and neighbour, Philippe Noisette. He gave the new seedling to Noisette, who made more crosses and sent both seed and plants to his brother, Louis, who was a nurseryman in Paris. The first seedlings were called 'Rosier de Philippe Noisette', a long name that came to be shortened to 'Noisette'.

'Noisette Carnée' (syn. 'Blush Noisette') is still widely grown, and so too is the beautiful 'Madame Alfred Carrière', one of the few climbing roses that can tolerate being grown against a north-facing wall.

Bourbon roses also made their appearance during this period. These began as a cross between *R. × odorata* 'Pallida', the old blush China rose, and *R. × damascena* var. *semperflorens*, the autumn damask rose, found growing in rose hedges on the Île de Bourbon (now called Réunion), an island in the Indian Ocean. Many of these shrub roses are still available, including 'Louise Odier' (syn. 'L'Ouche', 'Madame de Stella'), 'Souvenir de la Malmaison' (syn. 'Queen of Beauty and Fragrance') and the much-prized, thornless 'Zéphirine Drouhin'.

The modern rose

Throughout the 19th century hybrid perpetuals were introduced as a result of breeding between Chinas, Portlands, Bourbons and noisettes. The birth of what is considered to be the first modern rose, the large-flowered or hybrid tea rose, took place in Lyon in France in 1867 with the introduction of Jean-Baptiste Guillot's 'La France'. These new breed of roses satisfied gardeners' demands for neat, repeat-flowering and truly hardy shrubs with elegant and delicate flowers.

In the mid-18th century a wild rambler, *R. multiflora*, had been introduced from Japan. In the hands of 19th-century breeders it was to become the parent of the numerous cluster-flowered or floribunda roses that are grown today.

Most rose breeders of the 20th century have concentrated their efforts on floribunda and large-flowered (hybrid tea) roses, in colours echoing current tastes in fashion. Since the late 1960s there has also been a steady increase in the number of smaller shrubs for tiny gardens, patios and pots.

At the same time, a new breed of roses, evocative of Dutch old masters and the romantic paintings of Pierre Joseph Redouté (1759–1840), has been introduced by the British rose grower David Austin. He has raised roses that may be described as some of the finest reproductions, growing no more than 1.2m/4ft tall but with all the charm and scent of the classic roses of the past, crossing damasks and gallicas with modern shrub roses. Now owners of even the smallest garden may enjoy the delights of roses that the Empress Josephine would have considered for her garden.

■ LEFT

An outstanding modern shrub rose, 'L.D. Braithwaite' has all the charm of the old-fashioned roses.

■ OPPOSITE

'Graham Thomas' is one of the most popular of the modern shrub roses bred by David Austin in his series of "English" roses. It combines the form and fragrance of an old rose with a pure yellow colouring that 19th-century breeders could not achieve.

Roses Around the Garden

Roses are a favourite with gardening enthusiasts around the world. Even a solitary rose makes a wonderful focal point in any part of the garden. On the following pages we look at some of the planting methods that will inspire you to ever-greater creativity. A wide variety of other plants can be combined with roses to blend in subtly or to highlight a contrast. Roses can also be enjoyed indoors, cut fresh from the garden, or dried for longer-lasting beauty.

■ RIGHT
The centifolia hybrid 'Fantin-Latour' flowers for much of the summer. This rose was introduced about 1900 and named after Henri Fantin-Latour, the French flower painter.

Roses around the garden

Roses are often grown in dedicated beds or in areas of the garden devoted solely to them, but they are very versatile plants that can be used imaginatively all around the garden. The following pages show some of the interesting and beautiful ways in which roses can be used.

Some rose enthusiasts prefer to create a rose garden in which few other plants feature, but there is a risk that such a strategy will leave the garden looking bare for part of the year. Other gardeners are put off planting more roses simply because of the short period of interest with some types, especially the once-flowering climbers and ramblers and some of the species and old-fashioned roses.

By selecting the right rose varieties for your garden, however, and using them creatively, it is possible to enjoy all the charm and beauty of roses without sacrificing any of the delights of your garden, year round.

■ RIGHT
Use climbers and ramblers to clothe otherwise boring fences and walls. Even when flowering is over, the foliage will act as a pleasing green screen for the rest of summer and into autumn. Here 'Madame Alfred Carrière', which continues to flower intermittently into autumn, is doing a magnificent job enhancing a boundary.

■ ABOVE
The yellow floribunda shrub 'Chinatown' looks perfect in this mixed border.

■ ABOVE
The clever positioning of a rose with an urn can lend structure to the planting and provide a pleasing contrast of form. This is 'Golden Celebrations', a modern shrub.

Purists may prefer their roses unadulterated, but most gardeners appreciate other plants, too, and one plant can often be used to enhance another. A rambling rose such as 'Wedding Day' climbing through a flowering cherry will drape the branches with creamy white flowers a month or two after the cherry blossom is over, giving two displays instead of one.

Clematis are compatible with roses, and they are often used together. A late-flowering clematis growing through a climbing or rambling rose will double the flowering capacity of a given space. Alternatively, a clematis that flowers at the same time as the rose can provide a stunning contrast of colours. Prune the clematis hard back in early spring.

Roses can be used together with other shrubs in shrub or mixed borders, and they can be used as hedges, flowering ground cover or even as container plants. In recent years breeders have created more versatile varieties with a wider range of uses and longer flowering periods, opening up many possibilities for using them all around the garden.

■ ABOVE
Climbing roses can soften and disguise harsh structures such as garden sheds. This is the fragrant and almost thornless 'Blush Rambler'.

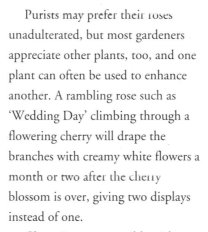

■ ABOVE
Shrub roses look perfectly in place in a shrub or mixed border, and ramblers, climbers or pillar roses can be grown up supports to give height to the bed.

Happy marriages

For some stunning effects, try interplanting your roses with other plants that make happy combinations of colour and form. Purists may consider that this detracts from the roses, but as a garden feature roses can be enhanced by what you plant with them.

Pansies (*Viola* spp.) provide a simple solution if you want to cover the ground between the roses, especially in winter and spring when the roses are not in leaf. In summer they will find it difficult to compete in the shade, except at the edge of the border. Polyanthus (primulas) are also useful for spring colour.

In summer, when the roses are in bloom, their companions need to be stronger and bolder plants. Annual grasses provide an eye-catching contrast and are easily planted among existing roses, but choose a variety of grass that does not grow taller than the rose. Lavenders (*Lavandula* spp.) and catmints (*Nepeta* spp.), with their blue, lavender or purple flowers, are popular companions, but they are permanent features in the bed, and the spacing of the roses should allow for both plants.

It is worth experimenting with the unexpected, such as yellow day lilies (*Hemerocallis* cvs.) with yellow roses or pink gypsophila (baby's breath) interplanted among pink roses.

Always bear in mind that for tiptop roses you will need to feed, spray and, with some roses, regularly deadhead them. Plants that make rose cultivation difficult may mean some sacrifice of quality of bloom.

■ LEFT
Shrub roses and even ramblers are ideal for mixed borders if they can be given space to grow to their full potential. In this mainly white border, the white ramblers 'Félicité et Perpétue', 'Bobbie James' and 'Adélaïde d'Orléans' blend in beautifully among the other plants.

■ OPPOSITE
Clematis make ideal partners for roses, and here one acts as a bridge between 'Madame Alfred Carrière' and 'Bobbie James'. Clematis can be chosen to flower at the same time or to extend the period of interest by blooming later. If the clematis is to grow through the rose itself, where its stems will become entwined, selecting a late-flowering variety, which will need to be cut back hard in early spring, will make the task of pruning easier.

Beautiful beds

Many roses, especially large-flowered (hybrid tea) and cluster-flowered (floribunda) varieties, look best when massed in a rose bed. Where space is unrestricted, whole beds of a single variety can look stunning, especially when fragrance matches the perfection of bloom. Beds of mixed roses can also be very pleasing, but for impact plant in groups of about five plants of each variety and select varieties that harmonize well in terms of size and habit as well as colour.

Rose beds are most appropriate in a formal rose garden, with rectangular or circular beds set into the lawn, ideally with pergolas or arches clothed with climbers and ramblers. This kind of garden is a rose lover's paradise, especially if it is set with suitably positioned seats surrounded by fragrance. Many enthusiasts willingly forgo other plants for such bliss and beauty.

Floribundas are ideal for beds designed to be viewed from a distance, where a mass of blooms over a long period is more important than the quality of individual flowers. Beds of large-flowered (hybrid tea) roses generally have less impact from a distance, and flowering can be more uneven, especially where there are many varieties in the same bed. This is irrelevant for those rose lovers who prefer to savour the beauty of individual blooms.

Many modern gardens are too small for formal rose beds set in a large lawn, but there is plenty of scope for patio beds. Choose low-growing floribunda varieties – these are sometimes described as patio roses – for small beds set into the patio. Patio and miniature roses are also ideal for raised beds, where they can replace seasonal bedding plants. Although the initial investment is greater, the money you save on seasonal bedding will recover the cost of the roses over a few seasons.

■ LEFT
Rose beds have more impact if they are densely planted. The rose in the foreground is the polyantha rose 'The Fairy', which bears profuse clusters of pale pink blooms from summer to autumn.

■ OPPOSITE
A formal rose garden is the ideal way to grow roses. Both visual impact and scent are concentrated, and it is a magical place to sit on a hot summer's day. Large rose beds such as this have space for many different kinds of rose, but even in a small rose garden it is important to use pergolas or frames for climbers to provide the essential element of height.

Border beauties

Roses are ideal border plants, whether they are grown in mixed plantings or in an area specifically dedicated to roses. Many varieties have a long flowering season that will out-perform most other flowering shrubs, and, of course, they contribute the special charm of their fragrance.

If limited space in your garden makes it impossible for you to create formal rose beds cut into the lawn, it is usually possible to create a rose border. Instead of filling the area with herbaceous plants, pack it with roses of all kinds and colours. The border will look spectacular in early and mid-summer and will continue to provide pockets of interest right through until autumn.

Use shrub roses and pillar roses at the back of the border, modern shrub roses and the taller floribundas towards the centre, and compact floribundas and large-flowered (hybrid tea) types towards the front, with some of the long-flowering ground-cover roses as an edging. A kaleidoscope of colour works best

with this kind of rose border and enables many varieties to be grown.

Rose borders are ideal for old-fashioned and modern shrub roses, many of which are too tall or bushy for formal rose beds. These roses also have a more informal shape, which is appropriate for a shrub border.

Use shrub roses to transform an existing shrub border that looks tired and rather dull, perhaps one that has large shrubs at the back that are grown largely for their foliage. Shrub roses planted in front of large, established shrubs will bring the border to life in summer, and the foliage behind makes a pleasing

backdrop against which to view the roses. Species roses, especially the tall-growing kinds such as *Rosa moyesii*, which is grown for its decorative hips, and *R. sericea* subsp. *omeiensis* f. *pteracantha* (syn. *R. omeiensis* f. *pteracantha*), the winged thorn rose, which is grown mainly for its spectacular thorns, are also ideal in this situation.

If there is no space for a formal rose garden or rose border, integrate as many roses as possible into a mixed border. If you can make the border a viewpoint from an arbour of roses, or from a sitting area framed by roses, so much the better.

■ RIGHT
A plain, dark green hedge makes a good background against which to view a rose border. Pale colours, such as the flowers of the shrub rose 'Dapple Dawn', show up particularly well.

■ LEFT

Use ramblers, climbers and other tall roses at the back of a rose border. This will take the eye right to the back of the border, and the extra height makes sure that the feature is a focal point, even from a distance.

■ ABOVE

Try to incorporate a sitting area in the garden where you can linger to admire your rose border. Frame it with fragrant roses, perhaps using climbing roses to create a sense of enclosure like this. Use roses as a unifying theme to link different parts of the garden.

Hedges and boundaries

Garden walls and fences are essentially functional – that is, they are there to define the boundaries of the garden, to keep in children and pets and to keep out intruders. For a rose lover they are also a wonderful opportunity to plant more roses.

Walls and fences represent golden opportunities for planting climbing and rambling roses. Climbers can be planted against tall walls, while ramblers are a better choice for lower walls and fences. Even tall climbers and ramblers will, however, spread horizontally along a fence if they cannot grow upwards.

Fix horizontal supports 45–60cm/18–24in apart and train as many shoots as possible along these. New shoots will grow from this framework of horizontal branches to cover most of the wall or fence; whereas if all the shoots are allowed to grow upwards most of the flowers will be bunched together at the top and then simply tumble down over each other.

■ RIGHT
To obtain extra height for the more vigorous roses a trellis can be erected on top of a wall. When well-trained, they will present a backdrop of colour against which to view the border in front and below.

A rose hedge

Although roses can make beautiful boundaries and are ideal for an internal dividing hedge within a garden, they will not provide the year-round sense of privacy that an evergreen hedge of, say, privet or yew will impart. The thorny stems will deter some intruders and animals, but a rose hedge is best regarded as an ornamental feature.

Given these limitations, roses can make some of the best flowering hedging, blooming for far longer than most shrubs, and they sometimes have the bonus of scent. Few other hedges can match the rose for colour, length of flowering period and fragrance. Traditional choices are *Rosa rugosa* (sometimes called the hedgehog rose) and its varieties, such as 'Scabrosa', or the hybrid musk roses 'Cornelia' and 'Penelope'.

All of these roses will make a hedge 1.2m/4ft or more tall. For a smaller hedge try 'Ballerina', a lower growing polyantha hybrid musk with pink-flushed white flowers. The hydrangea-like clusters of musk-scented flowers are borne over a long period throughout the summer.

■ BELOW

Brick walls make an ideal background against which to view climbing roses, and in return the flowers soften the harshness of too much brickwork.

Tall floribunda roses also make pretty hedges, although they are less substantial than the shrub roses already mentioned. For that reason, it is best to plant them in a double, staggered row. Pleasing varieties for this purpose are 'Eye Paint' (syn. 'Maceye', 'Tapis Persan'), which has red flowers with white centres,

'Margaret Merril' (syn. 'Harkuly'), which has fragrant white flowers, 'Masquerade', whose flowers change from yellow to pink to dark red, and 'Southampton' (syn. 'Susan Ann'), which has apricot-orange flowers.

A rose hedge will be informal in profile and should not be clipped to a neat outline with shears.

Remember that rose hedges must not be neglected and allowed to become overgrown, especially those that border a public footpath. Roses with long, thorny shoots that catch on passers-by soon lead to disputes. Plant the roses a little further into the garden and not right at the edge so that they do not overhang a path.

Carpets of colour

Roses sound unpromising as ground-cover plants, but there are varieties able to create a carpet of colour that will look beautiful all summer long. They could be used to transform an area of neglected ground or a steep bank that is difficult to cultivate.

Some of the older ground-cover roses can be disappointing – they can be too tall for a small area and their flowering season is sometimes short. These criticisms, however, cannot be levelled against many of the compact ground-cover roses that have been bred in recent years. These literally form a carpet of blooms.

Roses will not create an impenetrable barrier against weeds, as some of the more traditional evergreen ground-cover shrubs do, but weeds are least active while the roses are dormant and devoid of foliage. Roses can therefore be quite effective weed suppressors if the ground is thoroughly cleared of weeds before planting and then mulched. The best way to be sure of eliminating weeds is to plant the roses through a mulching sheet.

■ RIGHT
Rosa 'Suffolk' is one of the brightest ground-cover roses. It grows to approximately 45cm/1½ft tall and has a spread of about 1m/3ft.

The term "ground-cover rose" is used to describe varieties with very different habits. Some are, indeed, ground hugging, but others are relatively tall and arching. Some have a spread of about 60cm/2ft, while others may reach 3m/10ft or more across. If you are considering a ground-cover rose, always make sure that the size and growth habit are appropriate for your garden. All these roses have their place in the garden, but the right kind must be chosen for each situation. There are three broad categories into which most ground-cover roses fit, although a few fall between these main groupings.

First are the tall ground-cover roses with arching stems. This group includes 'Pink Bells' (syn. 'Poulbells') and 'Red Bells' (syn. 'Poulred'), which grow to little more than 1m/3ft tall but have a spread of about 1.2m/4ft or more. The plants are smothered in double flowers in mid- and late summer. Prune them like shrub roses, but concentrate on shortening any branches that want to grow vertically.

The second group contains tall ground-cover roses that are almost as wide as they are tall. 'Rosy Cushion' (syn. 'Interall'), which has single, pink flowers; 'Smarty' (syn.

'Intersmart'), which has single, rose-madder flowers; 'Surrey' (syn. 'Korlanum'), which has double, pink flowers carried over a long period; and 'Sussex' (syn. 'Poulave'), which has double, apricot-pink flowers, also borne over a long period, fall into this category. Prune them in the same way as those with arching stems.

The final group consists of those varieties that spread wider than their height and that usually creep along the ground. It includes such roses as 'Pink Flower Carpet' (syn. 'Flower Carpet', 'Noatraum'), which has double, bright pink flowers over a long period; 'Grouse' (syn. 'Immensee', 'Korimro', 'Lac Rose'), which has single, pale pink flowers in mid- to late summer and which grows to about 60cm/2ft high but spreads to 3m/10ft or more; 'Kent' (syn. 'Poulcov', 'Pyrenees', 'White Cover'), which bears semi-double, white flowers; and *R. × jacksonii* 'Max Graf' (syn. 'Max Graf'), which has single, pink flowers and which ultimately grows to about 2.4m/8ft across. Other good choices are 'Nozomi' (syn. 'Heideröslein'), which has single, white-flushed pink flowers; 'Pheasant' (syn. 'Heidekönigin', 'Kordapt'), which has double, pink flowers borne in mid- to late summer and spreads to about 3m/10ft; and 'Snow Carpet' (syn. 'Maccarpe'), which has double, creamy white flowers. All these require minimal pruning other than to shorten the longest stems to restrain their spread.

■ ABOVE
A traditional ground-cover rose, 'Grouse' carries sweetly scented, pale pink flowers and is useful for covering a bank.

Roses as cut flowers

Beautiful at all stages, roses are the archetypal flower arranger's flower. They look stunning as tightly scrolled buds, at the height of their elegance just before opening, or as voluptuous flowers. The colour range is probably unmatched by any other flower, whether you are looking for brilliant whites, delicate creams and pastels or strong, vibrant reds, yellows and oranges. They last well, both in water and in florist's foam, and they are, of course, the traditional choice for buttonholes.

Whether you are buying roses or cutting them from the garden, always choose those in the very best condition. Reputable florists, supermarkets and flower stalls take pride in their flowers, selling only good quality blooms and having the knowledge and experience to keep them that way.

If you are cutting roses from the garden, it is best to gather them as early in the day as possible, when

ROSES FOR ARRANGING

Most roses provide good cut flowers, but the following are some of the longest lasting.

Pink
'Blue Moon'
'City of London'
'Double Delight'
'Escapade'
'Hannah Gordon'
'Julia's Rose'
'My Choice'
'Paul Shirville'
'Royal Highness'
'Savoy Hotel'
'Sexy Rexy'
'The Queen Elizabeth'

Red
'Alec's Red'
'Alexander'
'Big Purple'
'Fragrant Cloud'
'Ingrid Bergman'
'Papa Meilland'
'Precious Platinum'
'Red Ace'
'Red Devil'
'Royal William'

Orange
'Just Joey'
'Peek A Boo'
'Rosemary Harkness'
'Whisky Mac'

Yellow
'Allgold'
'Anne Harkness'
'Arthur Bell'
'Dutch Gold'
'Grandpa Dickson'
'Peace'
'Princess Michael of Kent'
'Sheila's Perfume'

White
'Elina'
'Elizabeth Harkness'
'Iceberg'
'Margaret Merril'
'Pascali'
'Polar Star'

PREPARING ROSES FOR A VASE ARRANGEMENT

1 After choosing the vase, cut off any leaves that will fall below the water level, because these will rot and cause the water to become stagnant.

2 Use a very sharp knife or pair of scissors to cut the stem diagonally to ensure maximum uptake of water. If thorns have to be removed because the roses are being used in a bouquet, use sharp scissors to cut them off, but not too close to the stem.

3 Add a proprietary flower food to the water in the vase to prolong the life of cut flowers and help to keep the water in the vase clear. It is sometimes possible to revive wilted roses by cutting the stems very short.

plant tissues are at their most turgid after the night dew. To increase your options when arranging, cut them with as long a stem as possible, cutting just above a leaf joint. For the longest lived arrangements, they should be still in bud but with the sepals fully reflexed. Immediately on cutting, stand the stems in fresh, deep water until you are ready to arrange them.

If you are buying roses, make sure that they are well wrapped to avoid excess evaporation and to protect their delicate petals. For long

journeys, if practicable, it is best to put them in a bucket of water; alternatively, ask the retailer to cover the ends of the stems with damp paper. As soon as you reach home, give the flowers a long drink by standing them in deep, tepid water for at least an hour.

If you are arranging in water, begin by removing from the lower part of the stem all the leaves that would otherwise be below water. If left, they may rot, shortening the life of the arrangement and creating an unpleasant smell. Trim the base of

the stems with a slanting cut. This provides the maximum area for the uptake of water and makes the stems easier to insert in plastic or florist's foam. Rose stems should never be crushed with a hammer, as some people suggest. This method destroys the delicate plant cells and makes the stalk less efficient in taking up water. It also encourages the spread of bacterial infection.

Opinions also differ about rose thorns. Some writers suggest that they can be removed by scraping a knife down the stems or, if the stems

are ripe, by snapping off the thorns with the finger and thumb. However, research has shown that bacteria may invade the gases left in the stem where the thorns are cut off, so it is better to remove the thorns only if the roses are going to be carried in a posy or bouquet when they might prick someone's hands.

Bacteria block the stems and cause the drooping heads so often experienced with shop-bought roses. You can avoid this problem by always using scrupulously clean vases, removing all leaves below the water level and adding commercially formulated flower food. This simple powder contains the correct amount of a mild and completely harmless disinfectant, which inhibits bacterial growth, together with the sugar that feeds the roses and encourages the flowers to mature and open. If flower flood is added to the water it is unnecessary to change it, but it may need topping up in warm weather. Although many people have their own recipes for increasing the longevity of cut roses – lemonade, aspirin, household bleach and so on – flower food is by far the most successful way of keeping roses at their best for longer.

For arrangements made using plastic foam, make holes for the rose and other stems with a wooden skewer. If you push the rose stem straight into the foam, particles of foam may become lodged in the base of the stem and prevent good water uptake, causing premature wilting. While arrangements in plastic foam often have great visual impact, they are usually shorter lived because it is impossible to feed the flowers after arranging. It is, however, possible to keep the arrangement fresh by periodically spraying with distilled water at room temperature.

If rose heads have wilted, either because of a bacterial infection or an airlock somewhere in the stem, it may be possible to revive them by wrapping them in strong paper and standing the stems in deep, tepid water for several hours, after first cutting at least 5cm/2in from the end of each stem. If this treatment fails, even more drastic action will be needed, and the roses will have to be cut very short in order to perk up their drooping heads.

Roses as dried flowers

■ BELOW
Drying roses at home is not difficult and it
is a wonderful way to preserve the beauty
of the flowers.

People have always wanted preserve the beautiful flowers and sweet scent of roses, and they have therefore been dried for as long as they have been cultivated. Rose petals have been used in pot-pourri or the whole stems in decorative arrangements when fresh flowers were scarce. The Elizabethans preserved roses by immersing them completely in dry sand and keeping them warm until all the moisture had been drawn out. In Victorian times, when houses were heated from open coal fires, which shortened the lives of fresh blooms, intricate dried arrangements were painstakingly created and then covered in glass domes to keep them free of dust. These rather contrived designs have lost their appeal in favour of looser, more natural arrangements, and contemporary designs using dried flowers have achieved new popularity.

The latest commercial method for drying roses is freeze-drying. The technique takes up to two weeks and requires specialized freezers, and it is therefore rather expensive, but the results are stunning. Dried roses retain all their original intensity of colour and, in some cases, even their fragrance. Freeze-dried flowers last for about five years before they begin to fade or disintegrate.

Air-drying is the most popular way of preserving roses at home. It is best for buds that are just about to open but still have their bud shape. They need to be hung somewhere that is well-ventilated, warm, dry and dark for a couple of weeks – a large airing-cupboard would be ideal. String them together washing-line-style to speed up the process and prevent any moisture being trapped between the flowers. Once they are completely dry, handle with care as the stems will be very brittle.

The petals will now have a delicate, faded tone. Try displaying a tight bunch of rosebuds packed together in a small terracotta pot for maximum impact. A gentle blow on

the lowest setting of a hair-drier will usually be sufficient to remove most of the dust that settles on them.

Drying roses in a microwave oven is suitable for arrangements requiring short stems. Lay the flowers on greaseproof paper and put them into the microwave, which should be switched to its lowest setting. The roses will take only a very short time, and you should check them every minute to prevent over-cooking.

The third method is to use a desiccant such as silica gel, available from chemists and craft shops, or fine sand. Some silica gels change colour as they absorb the moisture from the plant material. A desiccant is suitable for drying single flowers.

Classifying and Identifying Roses

Rose classification has never been an exact science. Although the groups appear to be precisely defined horticulturally, the groupings are actually devised for the convenience of the gardener. Based on flowering patterns and habit of growth, the main groups are wild or species roses, old garden roses, early hybrids of European and Oriental roses, and modern roses.

■ RIGHT
'Bobbie James' is a vigorous rambling rose with sweetly scented small white flowers.

Classifying and identifying roses

Over the years hybridization has made the botanical classification of roses complex, and it is more useful for gardeners to group them by growth and flowering habit. There are several thousand documented roses, including original species and scores of hybrids that have been bred during the last four centuries. Many more new rose varieties are introduced every year, and older hybrids are being rediscovered all over the world.

The world's rose societies have developed a horticultural classification that is broadly based on habit of growth and flowering patterns, and the main groups are wild or species roses, old garden roses,

early hybrids of European and Oriental roses, and modern roses. In 1971 the World Federation of Rose Societies reclassified both ancient and modern roses into more clearly defined garden groups. Broadly speaking, the era of the modern rose began in 1867 with the introduction of the first hybrid tea (large-flowered) rose, 'La France', by the French grower Jean-Baptiste Guillot. This rose is still available from one or two specialist nurseries.

The categories described here are broadly accepted by the rose growing community, but there will always be a few plants included in one group that some growers may feel belong rightly in one of the others.

Wild or species roses

This group includes the species and those roses that are hybrids of them with features that clearly identify them as offspring of a particular species. They are generally vigorous and produce one flush of single flowers in early summer, often followed by decorative hips. One of the most popular wild rose hybrids is 'Dupontii' which has beautiful white flowers with golden stamens.

Old roses

When it comes to classifying old roses there are no hard-and-fast rules. Even the term "old rose" is itself rather misleading, as this group often includes some modern hybrids that fit into this category as they have the grace and flower form that are associated with older roses.

With a few exceptions, old garden roses are the albas, gallicas, damasks, centifolias and moss roses, along with the Scotch or burnet roses (derived from *R. pimpinellifolia*) and the sweet briars (derived from *R. rubiginosa*).

■ LEFT
R. rugosa has distinctive wrinked leaves and bright pink flowers, followed in autumn by large, rounded red hips.

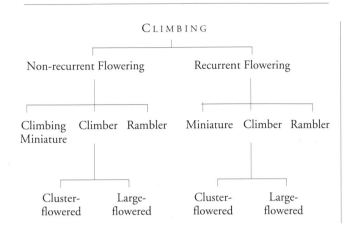

CLIMBING

- Non-recurrent Flowering
  - Climbing Miniature
  - Climber
    - Cluster-flowered
    - Large-flowered
  - Rambler
- Recurrent Flowering
  - Miniature
  - Climber
    - Cluster-flowered
    - Large-flowered
  - Rambler

NON-CLIMBING

- Non-recurrent Flowering
  - Ground-cover
  - Shrub
    - Cluster-flowered
      - Dwarf Cluster-flowered
    - Large-flowered
- Recurrent Flowering
  - Miniature
    - Polyantha
  - Bush
  - Shrub
    - Cluster-flowered
    - Large-flowered
  - Ground-cover
    - Cluster-flowered
    - Large-flowered

These shrubs, many of them intensely fragrant, vary considerably in size, habit, flower shape and colour.

The polyanthas – compact, hardy and relatively thornless shrubs and climbers – are also often (although not invariably) included with the old roses.

Early hybrids

The early European and Oriental hybrids are mostly repeat-flowering roses derived from crossings with *R. chinensis*, and include Chinas, Portlands, noisettes, Bourbons, tea roses and hybrid perpetuals.

■ RIGHT
The Bourbon rose 'Louise Odier' was introduced in 1851. It is still grown for its strongly scented, warm-pink flowers.

Alba
These large, long-lived, strong-growing roses have attractive grey-green foliage and produce a single flush of white or pale pink flowers in mid-summer. They will tolerate poor soil. Popular alba roses include 'Königin von Dänemark' (syn. 'Belle Courtisane') and 'Great Maiden's Blush' (syn. 'Cuisse de Nymphe').

Bourbon
A vigorous, usually repeat-flowering, rose which can also be trained as short climber. Some grow to over 3m/10ft, others remain low-growing and shrubby. Bourbon roses are sweetly scented and derive from a damask × China cross. 'Souvenir de la Malmaison' and 'Madame Isaac Pereire' are amongst the best known.

Centifolia
These lax shrubs have large, many-petalled flowers which weigh down the arching stems. The leaves are large, drooping and sometimes wrinkled. Centifolias are sometimes referred to as cabbage, Provence or Holland roses. A typical centifolia is *R. × centifolia* 'Cristata' (syn. 'Chapeau de Napoléon').

Rosa odorata 'Mutabilis' is a China rose of unknown origin which displays beautifully subtle changes of colour as it ages.

Hybrid Perpetual

The vigorous shrubs, usually repeat-flowering, initially grow upright. Legginess tends to develop later, but the problem may be overcome by pegging down the overlong shoots. Popular hybrid perpetuals are 'Mrs John Laing' and 'Frau Karl Druschki' (syn. 'Reine des Neiges', 'Snow Queen', 'White American Beauty').

Moss

Closely allied to the centifolia roses, moss roses arose as sports of centifolias and damasks, but they are distinguished by the characteristic mossy growth on their stems and calyces. The old black rose 'Nuits de Young' has the typical brownish-green mossing on the stems.

Noisette

The first noisette rose was grown in Charleston, South Carolina in the early 1800s. It is believed to have resulted from a cross between the old blush China rose (*R.* × *odorata* 'Pallida') with a musk rose, *R. moschata*. These climbing roses usually have glossy leaves and fairly smooth stems. 'Madame Alfred Carrière', one of the best known and most widely grown of all climbing roses, is a noisette.

China

China roses are dainty, repeat-flowering shrubs of light, open habit, with small, scented flowers and leaves. A few are grown under glass in cold climates, since they are not fully hardy. 'Irène Watts', which has large, double flowers in a delicate shade of pink, is a China rose.

Damask

The lax, spreading, medium-sized to large shrubs usually bear highly scented flowers in clear colours. The leaves are typically greyish-green and have downy undersides. 'Madame Hardy', which has fully double, fragrant, white flowers, is among the most widely grown damask roses.

Gallica

Usually upright, although occasionally spreading, the compact shrubs have coarse leaves and flowers in deep shades of pink, rich crimson and purple. The group includes some striped roses. The lovely roses 'Tuscany Superb' and 'Charles de Mills' are in this group.

Hybrid Musk

Similar to the modern shrub rose, these have *R. moschata*, the musk rose, in their make-up. These roses were first bred between 1913 and 1926. One of the earliest introductions, the creamy white flowered 'Moonlight' (introduced in 1913) is still available.

Polyantha

This group of roses is now more or less obsolete. They are tough and repeat flowering and produce trusses of small flowers. The beautiful rose 'Cécile Brünner' (syn. 'Mignon', 'Sweetheart Rose') is sometimes classified as a polyantha. These are the forebears of the modern cluster-flowered (floribunda) roses.

Portland

The result of a damask × gallica cross, Portland roses are similar to the Bourbon roses but repeat more reliably and make small plants. 'Madame Knorr' (syn. 'Comte de Chambord'), introduced in 1860, is still available and widely grown.

Rugosa

These tough, vigorous and very hardy plants have crinkled foliage and single to double flowers, which are succeeded by large, tomato-like hips.

The rugosas originated in the Far East and have not been used extensively in rose breeding in the West. Nevertheless, rugosa roses are easy to grow and are valued for their robust constitution and their ability to tolerate some shade. They can be used as hedging, as specimens, in the border or in light woodland. 'Blanche Double de Coubert', which was introduced as long ago as 1892, is still popular.

Scotch Roses

These roses are dense shrubs with *R. pimpinellifolia* (syn. *R. spinosissima*), the burnet or Scots rose, in their make-up. The stems are often prickly. 'Frühlingsmorgen' (syn. 'Spring Morning') is a pimpinellifolia hybrid.

Tea

The slender-stemmed tea roses flower repeatedly throughout the summer, although they are often weak-growing shrubs which may need the protection of glasshouses in cold climates. Slender, pointed buds are a feature of many of the modern, large-flowered roses that are derived from them and that are often known as hybrid teas.

WHAT'S IN A NAME?

Although almost thirty years have elapsed since the new classifications were recommended, both gardeners and growers tend to cling to the old names with which most are familiar. In many catalogues, on labels in rose gardens and in everyday conversation, cluster-flowered roses are still likely to be described as floribundas and large-flowered roses referred to as hybrid teas. Both terms are used for each type of rose in this book.

In addition to what might be regarded as the "official" categories, catalogues sometimes describe varieties as "patio roses". These are low-growing cluster-flowered (floribunda) roses that are suitable for patio beds or containers. Some of the smaller patio roses are similar in size to the largest miniatures.

Catalogues sometimes use a grower's code name for the variety as well as the name under which it is widely known and distributed. For example, 'Sexy Rexy' is the selling name of 'Macrexy' (which was bred by McGredy), and 'Paul Shirville' is the selling name of 'Harqueterwife' (which was bred by Harkness). The breeder's name is a way of identifying a variety if the local name is changed when the rose is sold in different countries. It is also the name likely to be used during early trials, before the variety is released to the public.

■ BELOW
Ground-cover roses such as 'Red Bells'
have a low, spreading habit and form
dome-like mounds.

Modern roses

The suggestion that rose groupings are devised for the convenience of gardeners and are of little significance botanically is well illustrated by the categories used for modern roses. Some cluster-flowered (floribunda) roses – for instance, 'Chinatown' – are potentially large bushes that some growers prefer to define as shrub roses and treat accordingly. Some large-flowered (hybrid tea) roses have a tendency to produce smaller buds around the main bud, showing some of the characteristics of the cluster-flowered rose.

Modern roses are deciduous shrubs that bear their flowers on wood produced during the current season and on shoots emerging from the previous year's wood. In warm climates roses will grow virtually continuously, but in cold climates there is a period of winter dormancy. Roses generally benefit from pruning when they are dormant, usually early spring, to maintain a high proportion of young, productive growth.

Modern shrub roses are usually large, repeat-flowering shrubs that were bred after the advent of large-flowered (hybrid tea) and cluster-flowered (floribunda) roses.

Cluster-flowered Roses

Also known as floribundas. These sometimes large shrubs bear single to fully double flowers in clusters. The flowers usually open flat to reveal their stamens, producing dome-shaped heads. Cluster-flowered roses are a diverse group and can have a wide variety of uses around the garden: some can be grown as hedges or as specimens, whereas others are suitable for bedding or more informal planting schemes.

Dwarf Cluster-flowered Bush Roses

Also sometimes known as patio roses. Dwarf cluster-flowered bush roses are similar in style to cluster-flowered roses, but they are much smaller. Although they were bred specifically to be grown in containers, they are also good plants for patio beds, borders and low hedges.

Ground-cover Roses

Roses with a lax, trailing habit, they are closely allied to ramblers but are generally much smaller. Many have single flowers. Ground-cover roses can be used to cover banks or trail from raised beds. They are sometimes available as weeping standards.

Large-flowered Roses

Also known as hybrid teas. The shrubs are characterized by large flowers, usually carried singly but which sometimes grow in small clusters. They open from pointed buds usually to a high-centred, round or urn-shaped flower. Typically, the flowers are fully double, although there are a few varieties with single flowers. Many are suitable for bedding or mixed planting. A few large-flowered roses are stiff, rather gaunt plants, which are best grown solely for cut flowers.

Miniature Roses

These are compact plants, usually under 30cm/1ft high, carrying sprays of tiny flowers, which are often scentless. Miniature roses are versatile plants and can be grown in containers, to edge a border or in a rock garden. They are also sometimes sold as pot plants.

■ BELOW
The rich crimson 'Parkdirektor Riggers' is a good rose for growing up a pillar. It bears repeated flushes of crimson flowers.

Climbing roses

Unlike bush roses, climbing roses cannot be conveniently ascribed to distinct groups. They have a variety of ancestors and varying growth habits, which make them suitable for different garden uses. Habit – the way a rose (or any plant) grows – should be as important a consideration as flower colour and scent when choosing a rose for the garden but, unfortunately, is all too often overlooked. This section will help avoid some of the pitfalls.

Most climbing roses are deciduous, although a few, such as the vigorous 'Mermaid' and 'Albéric Barbier', are evergreen or semi-evergreen. In botanical and gardening terms they are divided into ramblers and climbers.

Rambling Roses

The rambling roses that are closely related to their wild ancestors – 'Seagull', 'Rambling Rector' and 'Wedding Day', for example – produce large trusses of small, single, usually highly fragrant flowers in a single flush around mid-summer on slender, flexible stems. Some are extremely vigorous indeed and must be given plenty of room.

A few rambling roses, however, such as 'Albertine', produce larger flowers, also in clusters, on stiffer, less flexible stems. All ramblers flower on wood that was produced the previous year. Some flower reliably on older wood. In some cases decorative hips follow in the autumn. After flowering, most produce large quantities of new wood from around the base of the plant. Ramblers usually need ample space to give of their best and are suitable for informal planting in a wild garden. They do not lend themselves to formal planting schemes and are less suitable than climbers for growing against walls.

Climbing Roses

This group of roses usually flowers twice, the first flush appearing around mid-summer, the second, lesser flush

in early autumn. Some, such as 'Mermaid', have a main flush in summer followed by spasmodic flowering right up until the first frosts of winter. These flowers are produced in small trusses on the current season's growth.

Most roses are thorny. In some cases – 'Albertine' and 'Mermaid', for example – the thorns are viciously sharp, but other roses – for example, 'Zéphirine Drouhin' and 'Climbing Iceberg' – have stems which are virtually thornless.

Some climbing roses are more tolerant of shade than bush roses, reflecting the fact that many of the wild roses from which they are descended were woodland plants.

In response to the needs of gardeners with only limited space, most climbers that have been bred since 1949 are only moderately vigorous and in many cases grow no more than 5m/16½ft tall. Some have been developed to reach no more than 2.4m/8ft or less, and miniature climbers seldom exceed 2.1m/7ft.

Extensive breeding and cross-breeding by modern rose breeders have meant that all the varied flower forms of bush roses can be found among climbing roses, which gives the gardener extra choice.

Flower shape

Most modern roses have many petals. Single flowers have eight or fewer petals; semi-double ones have 8–20 petals; double flowers have 20 or more petals, and fully double ones have 30 or more. Because of the double nature of most rose flowers and the sterility (or part sterility) of many, pollination in the garden seldom takes place, and hips are generally not produced.

Modern roses have stronger, richer colours than old roses, and their thicker petals are generally more rain resistant. They also have a longer flowering season, either in two distinct flushes (one around mid-summer, the other in late summer to autumn) or flower more or less continuously from summer until the first frosts.

Although this is a guide only, the flower shapes of roses are generally described as follows.

Flat

Single (with five petals) or semi-double (with ten petals) flowers open virtually flat, often revealing a prominent boss of stamens. A good example of an old rose with flat flowers is 'Dupontii'.

Cupped

Single to semi-double flowers with incurving petals that form a shallow to deep cup shape around the central stamens. *R. xanthina* 'Canary Bird' has beautiful yellow cupped flowers.

Rounded

Double or fully double flowers, with a rounded outline, formed by overlapping petals, which are usually of equal size and which form a bowl-shaped outline. 'Madame Grégoire Staechelin' (syn. 'Spanish Beauty') is a climbing rose with fully double rounded flowers.

Rosette

The low-centred, almost flat, semi- to fully double flowers are packed with many short, overlapping petals of uneven size. 'William Lobb' (syn. 'Duchesse d'Istrie'), first introduced in 1855, has large, double, rosette flowers.

Quartered rosette

Similar to the double or fully double rosette, but the petals are arranged in distinctive quarters within the flower. One of the best known roses with such flowers is 'Souvenir de la Malmaison', which bears scented, soft pink flowers.

Flower shapes: rosette, quartered rosette
and pompon.

Pompon

Double or fully double flowers,
generally borne in clusters, are small,
rounded and packed with many tiny
petals. 'Pompon de Paris' (syn. *R.
chinensis* 'Minima', 'Rouletii') is one
of the smallest miniature roses but
has – as its name suggests – beautiful
pompon flowers.

High-pointed

The semi- to fully double flowers
have a tight, high-pointed centre, as
seen in many large-flowered (hybrid
tea) roses. The patio rose 'Cider Cup'
(syn. 'Dicladida') has high-pointed
flowers in an unusual warm apricot-
pink colour.

Urn-shaped

Semi- to fully double blooms with
incurved inner petals and more
spreading outer petals. This is the
characteristic shape of China and tea
roses, which have long, slender,
elegant buds that open to high-centred
or urn-shaped flowers. A classic
example of a China rose with urn-
shaped flowers is 'Cécile Brünner'.

Flower shapes: urn-shaped and
high-pointed.

Old Roses

The history of old roses

What is an 'old' rose? Some people define an old rose as one that was developed and grown before World War I (1914–18), but the answer to this deceptively simple question is unfortunately not quite as clear cut as that straightforward definition would suggest. Indeed, it would be simpler to turn it on its head and ask what a 'modern' rose is. By common consent, modern roses are the large-flowered (hybrid tea) and cluster-flowered (floribunda) roses that until recently made up the majority of roses in commerce. In fact, however, 'La France', which is recognized as the first hybrid tea, appeared as long ago as 1867. Many of the so-called old roses are actually much younger than 'La France'.

Nowadays, the long and stately catalogue of old roses consists of a number of distinct groups: albas, Bourbons, centifolias, Chinas, hybrid perpetuals, damasks, gallicas, mosses, Portlands and teas. We might also include in the category the attendant species (or wild) roses, rugosas, hybrid musks, modern shrub roses and 'English' roses.

Exactly when many of the individual groups arose is not known, but what is certain is that one of the first to be grown in gardens that is recognizable today is *Rosa gallica*. The influence of this rose is present in nearly all of the roses that are still firm favourites today. A cross between *R. gallica* and *R. phoenicia* (or possibly *R. moschata*) resulted in *R. × damascena*, the original damask. Further crosses and back-crosses occurred, and from this emerged the albas. Pliny the Younger (AD 61–112), the great Roman letter writer, grew various kinds at his two country villas, and the Romans introduced some of them into the rest

■ OPPOSITE

The tall perennial *Campanula lactiflora* blends happily with many of the old roses, which can be allowed to flop in the mixed border.

■ BELOW

One of the most ancient roses, *R.* × *odorata* 'Pallida' (the old blush China rose) also has one of the longest flowering seasons.

■ LEFT

A moss rose, showing the characteristic mossy stems and calyces.

used as an ingredient in medicines) or as the Provins rose (after the area of France where it was grown for perfume production).

In England its flower was adopted as the badge of the House of Lancaster. The rival House of York used *R. × alba* 'Alba Semiplena' (or perhaps the British native *R. arvensis*), and Henry VII merged the two, heraldically speaking, to form the Tudor rose. Later, the double *R. × alba* 'Alba Maxima' became the emblem of Bonnie Prince Charlie.

Because the rose is the quintessential flower of summer, the Italian painter Sandro Botticelli (c.1444–1510) used some artistic licence when he painted *Primavera* – she who embodies spring – wearing a dress decorated with roses. She also carries a bouquet of the same flowers.

Centifolias – sometimes called cabbage roses – were so common in the Netherlands and France that they were also known as Holland or Provence roses. They often appear in 17th-century Dutch paintings.

The common moss rose, *R. × centifolia* 'Mucosa', which is distinguished by its mossy stems and calyces (the green segments that enclose the unopened bud), is a sport (spontaneous mutation) of a

of their Western empire. Pliny also grew a rose he described as centifolia (literally, with a hundred leaves, although meaning petals), but this is thought to be a different rose from the centifolias we know today, which did not evolve until the 16th century.

The rose retained its supremacy throughout the Middle Ages and the Renaissance, acquiring both sacred and secular resonances. It was one of the celebrated plants in the gardens of

Islam, since it was believed to have been created from a bead of perspiration on the brow of Mohammed, and roses are recorded growing in the palace garden in Constantinople in the 16th century. In medieval Europe roses came to be associated both with the Holy Spirit and the Virgin Mary. *R. gallica* var. *officinalis* (syn. *R. officinalis*) had a commercial value and was known as the apothecary's rose (because it was

■ BELOW
Venus, the patroness of flower gardens as well as the goddess of love, oversees a mass planting of roses.

centifolia that was first noticed about 1720. At around the same time China and tea roses began to arrive in Europe from the Far East. These roses were not hardy in north European climates and initially attracted little interest other than as novelties, but they contributed significantly to the explosion in rose breeding that occurred in the 19th century. Unfortunately, little is known of the history of these plants before their arrival in Europe.

The value of the tea and China roses as breeding material lay not only in their elegance, scent and colour, but in the fact that they have an extended flowering season. Some produce two distinct flushes and others flower virtually non-stop throughout summer. Earlier European groups produce one glorious crop of flowers in mid-summer, then do not flower again.

■ BELOW

In late summer the soft tones of border
phlox blend beautifully with old roses.

■ RIGHT
The hybrid musk rose 'Penelope' is a
glorious sight in full bloom.

■ RIGHT
The hybrid musk rose 'Penelope' is a
glorious sight in full bloom.

The so-called autumn damask rose,
R. × *damascena* var. *semperflorens*,
sometimes called 'Quatre Saisons', is
an exception that squeezes out a few
more blooms in autumn. Crosses
between this and the China roses
resulted in the repeat-flowering
Bourbon and Portland roses that
became the new stars in the rose
firmament. Further crossbreeding led
to the hybrid perpetuals, which have
a more dependable second flush. All
of the modern repeat-flowering roses
owe this characteristic to the Chinas.

It was in France in the 19th
century that rose breeding began in
earnest, and it is from this period on
that most of the old roses we still
grow today were bred. Their names
read like a roll call of the leading
personalities and society beauties of
the day: the Duc de Guise, Président
de Sèze, the Duchesse de Montebello
and Madame Hardy.

The vogue was started by the
interest, indeed the passion, of the
empress Joséphine (1763–1814). At
her country house of Malmaison she
created what was virtually the first
rose garden. Her 250 plants were
recorded for posterity by the great
botanical artist Pierre Joseph
Redouté. This was probably the rose's
heyday – at least before the

development of the hybrid teas and
floribundas – but a number of mainly
British rosarians kept the torch
glowing into the 20th century.
Among the prime movers were
Gertrude Jekyll and the Reverend
Pemberton, who created the group of
roses called hybrid musks, probably
by crossing a musk rose with a tea or
China rose. Vita Sackville-West grew
many old roses in her garden at
Sissinghurst and also fostered interest

in them through her writings. More
recently, so-called 'English' roses were
developed from the late 1950s
onwards by the rose breeder David
Austin, who wanted to combine the
flower types found in old roses with
the repeat-flowering habit of large-
flowered (hybrid tea) and cluster-
flowered (floribunda) roses. They are
mainly compact shrubs that fit well
into a small garden.

Old roses in the garden

Generally tough, hardy and free-flowering, old roses are splendid subjects for the garden, and all lend themselves to an informal, mixed, cottage style of planting that uses other shrubs, hardy perennials and summer bulbs. Many make large, rangy plants that may need some form of support, or you can allow them to flop over gracefully into neighbouring shrubs. There are some gallicas, Chinas and teas, however, that grow no larger than about 1.2m/4ft and that are suitable for the smallest gardens.

Flower colours of the European types include white, all shades of pink, dusky red, crimson and purple. Some flowers, such as *Rosa gallica* 'Versicolor' (sometimes known as *Rosa mundi*) and the Bourbon 'Variegata di Bologna', are striped in a combination of these colours. Genes from the China and tea roses have widened the range to include yellow and soft orange, but on the whole the palette is one that we associate with old silks, chintzes and velvets. In some flowers the colour changes as the flower ages, a good example being the gallica 'Belle de Crécy', whose rich, lilac-coloured flowers gradually pale into tones of dove-grey. On the whole, therefore, it is best to keep old roses away from other flowers that have strong, clear colours, although for a bold contrast you could try the rich purple gallicas 'Cardinal de Richelieu' and 'Tuscany Superb' with a sulphur-yellow *Achillea* such as 'Gold Plate'.

Otherwise, for strong contrasts, it is probably better to think in terms of form than of colour. The geometric

■ LEFT
A ceanothus supports an old rose and a late-flowering clematis.

■ OPPOSITE
A spectacular mass planting: a vigorous mock orange (*Philadelphus* spp.) forms the backdrop, while a mature Bourbon spreads its arching canes accommodatingly to fill the centre ground. Reliable hardy geraniums and pinks (*Dianthus*) grow at their feet.

■ BELOW
Shades of blue always provide a perfect foil
for soft-pink roses such as the centifolia
'De Meaux'.

shapes of plants like alliums and the
upright form of foxgloves (*Digitalis*
spp.) are the perfect foil to the laxer
roses. For a less spiky, more
integrated effect you could use easy
border perennials, such as hardy
geraniums, lady's mantle (*Alchemilla*

mollis) or catmint (*Nepeta* spp.).
All of these plants will blend well
with most old roses. Clouds of
gypsophila, such as *G. paniculata*
(baby's breath), or bronze fennel
(*Foeniculum vulgare* 'Purpureum')
will further soften the edges.

If you are still concerned about
colour clashes, add a few grey-leaved
plants such as artemisia, especially *A.
lactiflora* (white mugwort), or lambs'
ears (*Stachys byzantina*; syn. *S.
olympica*), sage (*Salvia officinalis*) and
Brachyglottis laxifolius (formerly

■ RIGHT
The vibrant red hips of *R. moyesii* are a stunning contrast with the purple flowers of *Thalictrum aquilegiifolium.*

Senecio) Dunedin Group 'Sunshine', although you will have to remove the rather ugly, daisy-flowers from the brachyglottis. In a large border underplant a tall-growing rose, such as the alba 'Great Maiden's Blush', with a hosta. The huge leaves of *H. sieboldiana* var. *elegans* would provide a sumptuous quilted cushion against which the roses could rest. A traditional edging would be tightly clipped box (*Buxus sempervirens* 'Suffruticosa'), but lavender, rosemary or the curry plant (*Helichrysum italicum*; syn. *H. angustifolium*) are more informal but equally attractive.

Apart from the beauty of the flowers, and perhaps even above that, roses are prized for their fragrance. This can range from the delicate tang of a modern shrub such as 'Nevada', which is more apparent when it is wafted on the air from a distance than close to, to the rich, crushed-berry scent of 'Madame Isaac Pereire'.

Roses are indispensable for a scented border. To create a pot-pourri of scents, provide a backdrop of mock orange (*Philadelphus* spp.), the flowering of which will coincide with the main summer flush of roses. Underplant with old-fashioned pinks (*Dianthus* spp.), such as the clove-scented 'Gran's Favourite', and try to include the heady fragrance of the regal lily (*Lilium regale*) or the incense-scented ornamental tobacco plant (*Nicotiana alata*). Remember that the scents will be heaviest at dusk, particularly after a light shower.

If your roses are the kind that produce a single crop of flowers, extend the season of interest by using them as props for late-flowering clematis. The rich purple *Clematis* 'Jackmanii', one of the most reliable, would look stunning entwined with the vibrant red hips of *Rosa moyesii* or any of the rugosa roses, particularly if the vibrant orange-red *Crocosmia* 'Lucifer', cannas, dahlias or orange annual nasturtiums (*Tropaeolum majus*) were planted to accompany them, bringing the curtain down on the rose season with a sensational chorus of colour.

Plant Catalogue

On the following pages the roses are organized alphabetically with the following categories.

Wild or species
Albas
Bourbons
Centifolias and mosses
Chinas and teas
Damasks
Gallicas
Other types

The height and spread that are included in the descriptions are those that the rose can be expected to achieve on maturity. They will vary, of course, depending on season, climate and soil type.

■ ABOVE
R. XANTHINA 'CANARY BIRD'

A wild or species rose of uncertain origin but assumed to be after 1907, the date of introduction of one of its possible parents, *R. xanthina* f. *spontanea*. It makes an arching shrub, 2.1m/7ft high and as much across or bigger. In late spring the canes are covered in cupped, single, scented, canary-yellow flowers with prominent stamens. The leaves are fern-like. *R. xanthina* 'Canary Bird', one of the earliest roses to flower, tolerates some shade.

Wild roses

■ RIGHT
'DUPONTII'

A wild or species rose hybrid, introduced around 1817 and known as the snowbush rose. It forms a spreading shrub 2.1m/7ft high and across. In summer the large, single, creamy white flowers open flat to reveal yellow stamens. The matt grey-green leaves are downy beneath. 'Dupontii' was grown by Empress Josephine.

Albas

■ BELOW

R. × ALBA 'ALBA MAXIMA'

This alba rose, dating from at least the 15th century, reaches a height of 1.8m/6ft with a spread of 1.5m/5ft. Somewhat untidy, cupped, double, very fragrant flowers, tinged pink on opening in summer but fading to creamy white, are followed by red hips. The foliage is grey-green. A rose of great historical significance, 'Alba Maxima' is sometimes known as the great white, Jacobite or Cheshire rose, while others consider it to be the white rose of York (see also R. × alba 'Alba Semiplena').

■ LEFT

R. × ALBA 'ALBA SEMIPLENA'

An alba rose, known in gardens since at least the 16th century. It is a graceful shrub with a height of 1.8m/6ft and a spread of 1.5m/5ft. In summer clusters of semi-double, very fragrant, milky-white flowers open flat to display prominent golden stamens. Red hips form in late summer to autumn. It has greyish-green foliage and is someimes grown as a hedge. 'Alba Semiplena' is usually held to be the white rose of York (see also R. × alba 'Alba Maxima').

■ LEFT
'CELESTE'

(syn. 'Celestial')
An alba rose with a lax, spreading habit that produces a shrub 1.8m/6ft or more high and across. The semi-double, sweetly scented, shell-pink flowers, with petals that appear almost transparent, are borne in summer and open flat to reveal prominent golden stamens. Red hips succeed them in autumn. The leaves are grey-green. The exact date of the introduction of 'Céleste' is unrecorded, but it is certainly a very old cultivar.

■ ABOVE
'FELICITE PARMENTIER'

An alba rose, known since about 1834, that grows into a compact shrub 1.2m/4ft high and across. In mid-summer it bears clusters of cup-shaped, highly scented, quartered, pale blush-pink flowers that open from primrose-yellow buds. The densely packed petals fade to almost white in hot sun and reflex to form a ball shape. The leaves are grey-green. One of the daintiest of the albas, 'Félicité Parmentier' would suit the smallest garden.

■ ABOVE
'KONIGIN VON DANEMARK'

(syn. 'Queen of Denmark', 'Belle Courtisane')
An alba rose, produced in 1826, that makes an elegant bush up to 1.5m/5ft high and 1.2m/4ft across. The luminous pink flowers, borne in summer, are fully double, quartered rosettes and richly scented, the colour fading to rose-pink as they mature. The leaves are pale greyish-green. It has one of the longest flowering seasons – up to six weeks – and the flowers are resistant to wet weather.

Bourbons

'LOUISE ODIER'

(syn. 'L'Ouche', 'Madame de Stella')
A Bourbon rose, introduced in 1851, that
makes a shrub 1.2m/4ft high and across.
From mid-summer to autumn, it produces
cupped, fully double, strongly scented,
lilac-tinted, warm-pink flowers. The leaves
are light grey-green. 'Louise Odier' has
slender shoots that can be supported on a
pillar or tripod.

'BOULE DE NEIGE'

A Bourbon rose, introduced in 1867,
growing to 1.5m/5ft high and 1.2m/4ft
across, although the weight of the flowers
may pull the slender stems further
sideways; it is best, therefore, with some
support. In summer and autumn clusters
of red-tinted buds open to fully double,
deeply cupped, strongly scented, white
flowers. The leaves are leathery and dark
green. 'Boule de Neige' (snowball) is so
named because as the flowers develop the
petals curl back to produce a ball shape.

■ BELOW
'BLAIRII NUMBER TWO'

A Bourbon rose, raised in 1845, that, if
untrained, will grow into an arching shrub
2.1m/7ft or more high and across. An
abundance of large, cupped, fully double,
sweetly scented flowers, borne in mid-
summer, are pale silvery pink with deeper
pink centres. The leaves, rough to the
touch, are matt dark green. 'Blairii
Number Two' produces few, if any, further
blooms in autumn. Its vigorous habit
makes it suitable for growing as a pyramid,
on a pergola or against a wall, where it can
reach 4m/13ft.

■ LEFT
'HONORINE DE BRABANT'

A Bourbon rose, of unknown origin, that
grows into a shrub about 1.8m/6ft high
and across. Its cupped, fully double,
strongly but sweetly scented flowers are
borne continuously from summer through
to autumn, the autumn flowering being
particularly good. The petals are pale pink,
spotted and striped with mauve and
crimson. The leaves are large and light
green. 'Honorine de Brabant' tolerates
poor soil. A sprawling rose, it is best with
some support and may be trained as a
short climber.

■ LEFT

'SOUVENIR DE LA MALMAISON'

A Bourbon rose, produced in 1843, growing into a dense shrub 1.5m/5ft high and across. Repeating throughout summer, it bears very fragrant, fully double, soft-pink flowers, which open to a quartered-rosette shape as they fade to pinkish-white. The leaves are large. The silk-textured flowers may be spoilt by wet weather. 'Souvenir de la Malmaison' is named in honour of Empress Josephine's famous garden at Malmaison.

■ RIGHT

'MADAME ISAAC PEREIRE'

A Bourbon rose, introduced in 1881, that grows into a large plant up to 2.1m/7ft high and 1.8m/6ft across. Borne from summer to autumn, the huge, richly fragrant, luminous, deep cerise-pink flowers open as quartered rosettes but become muddled as they mature, especially those of the first flush. The matt dark green leaves are abundant. 'Madame Isaac Pereire', one of the most strongly scented of all roses, is a vigorous plant that can also be trained as a climber.

Centifolias and mosses

■ RIGHT
R. × CENTIFOLIA 'CRISTATA'

(syn. 'Chapeau de Napoléon', 'Cristata')
A centifolia rose, bred in the 1820s. It is
sometimes incorrectly included among the moss
roses. It makes a graceful, slender-stemmed
shrub 1.5m/5ft high and 1.2m/4ft across. In
summer it produces drooping, cupped, fully
double, richly scented, deep silvery pink flowers,
which open flat and are sometimes
quartered. The foliage is abundant. It is
commonly known as the crested moss rose. The
name 'Chapeau de Napoléon' refers to the
unopened buds (see inset), which are three-
cornered, like the tricorn hat characteristically
worn by Napoleon Bonaparte.

■ LEFT
'FANTIN-LATOUR'

A centifolia rose, dating from around
1900, which makes a handsome, vase-
shaped shrub up to 2.1m/7ft high and
across. The flowers – cup-shaped, many-
petalled, lightly scented and blush-pink –
are borne in profusion over a long period
in summer. The petals reflex to reveal a
green button eye. The leaves are dark
green. Spraying against mildew may be
necessary in summer. 'Fantin-Latour' was
named in honour of the French flower
painter Henri Fantin-Latour (1836–1904).

■ LEFT

'NUITS DE YOUNG'

A moss rose, dating from 1845, which forms an upright then arching shrub 1.2m/4ft high and 1m/3ft across. Small, double, lightly scented, maroon-purple flowers open flat in summer to reveal golden stamens. The leaves are small and dark green. 'Nuits de Young' is valued for its unique dusky coloration; even the mossing of the stems and buds is dark reddish-brown. Its common name is old black rose.

■ RIGHT

'WILLIAM LOBB'

(syn. 'Duchesse d'Istrie')

A moss rose, introduced in 1855, which makes an upright but sprawling shrub 1.8m/6ft high and across. In mid-summer the large, double, rosette, heavily scented, magenta-purple flowers open from heavily mossed buds then fade to violet-grey. The tonal range of the flowers as they mature and fade is remarkable. The dark green leaves are abundant. 'William Lobb' is a vigorous rose that benefits from some support; it can be trained as a short climber on a pillar or against a wall.

Chinas and teas

■ RIGHT
'CECILE BRUNNER'

(syn. 'Mignon', 'Sweetheart Rose')
A China rose, which is sometimes classified
as a polyantha, introduced in 1880. It
makes a dainty bush about 1m/3ft high
and across. From summer to autumn
clusters of pointed buds open to urn-
shaped, delicately scented, pale pink
flowers that become more untidy as they
age. The leaves are pointed and sparse. The
buds are good for buttonholes, which may
explain the name 'Sweetheart Rose'.
'Cécile Brünner' is also sometimes known
as the Maltese rose. A climbing form and a
rare, white-flowered form are available.

■ RIGHT
'SOMBREUIL'

A climbing tea rose, introduced in 1850,
which will grow to 2.4m/8ft high and
1.5m/5ft across. From summer to autumn,
it produces flat, quartered-rosette, sweetly
scented flowers that are creamy white
tinged with pink as they age. The leaves
are mid-green. The flowers of 'Sombreuil'
can be spoilt by wet weather; nevertheless,
it is a rose of considerable distinction.

Damasks

'ISPAHAN'

(syn. 'Pompou des Princes', 'Rose d'Isfahan')

A damask rose, first recorded in 1832 but probably much older; it may be Persian in origin. It makes a compact shrub with a height of 1.2–1.5m/4–5ft and a spread of 1–1.2m/3–4ft. Large clusters of cupped, loosely double, reflexing, richly scented, clear pink flowers appear in summer. The grey-green foliage is attractive. 'Ispahan' has a longer flowering season than most other damask roses and is in bloom for up to six weeks.

'MADAME HARDY'

A damask rose, dating from 1867, which makes an elegant shrub up to 1.5m/5ft high and across. Cupped, fully double, quartered-rosette, strongly scented, white flowers are borne in profusion in summer, the petals reflexing to reveal a green button eye. The foliage is plentiful and matt light green. 'Madame Hardy' is generally considered to be one of the most sumptuous of old roses, although the flowers may be spoilt by rain.

Gallicas

■ RIGHT
'BELLE DE CRECY'

A gallica rose, bred before 1829, making a
bush about 1.2m/4ft high and 1m/3ft
across. The quartered-rosette, sweetly
scented flowers, produced in abundance in
mid-summer, open rich lilac-pink then
fade to paler pink. The leaves are dull
green. 'Belle de Crécy', although one of the
best gallicas, has a laxer habit than most,
and its arching stems may require support.

■ LEFT
'CHARLES DE MILLS'

(syn. 'Bizarre Triomphant')
A gallica rose which makes a compact shrub up to 1.2m/4ft in height with a spread of 1m/3ft or more. The fully double, quartered-rosette, moderately scented, rich crimson flowers, which are produced in summer, fade with grey and purple tones as they mature. The abundant foliage is matt dark green. 'Charles de Mills' has slender stems, which may need staking to support the large flowers. Its parentage and date of introduction are unknown.

■ OPPOSITE
'CARDINAL DE RICHELIEU'

A gallica rose, produced in 1840, which makes a compact bush 1.2m/4ft high and across and more if the stems are supported. In mid-summer it bears clusters of sumptuous, scented, dark maroon flowers, the petals of which are velvety in texture and reflex as the flowers age to form a ball shape. The stems are well covered with dark green leaves. 'Cardinal de Richelieu' needs good growing conditions and regular thinning of the old wood to give of its best. It can be used for hedging.

■ LEFT
'COMPLICATA'

Gallica rose that, as a free-standing shrub, grows to 2.4m/8ft high and wide. The single, cupped, sweetly scented flowers, produced in abundance in summer, are bright porcelain-pink and open wide to reveal white centres and golden stamens. The leaves are matt greyish-green and, unusually for a gallica, rather pointed. 'Complicata' is not typical of its group and is of uncertain origin. It can be used as a rambler among trees and shrubs or trained on a pillar. It tolerates light, sandy soils.

■ OPPOSITE

'DUCHESSE DE MONTEBELLO'

A gallica rose, bred before 1829, that
makes a spreading bush about 1.2m/4ft
high and across. The open-cupped, fully
double, sweetly fragrant flowers are soft
blush-pink. The foliage is light green.
'Duchesse de Montebello' is one of the
daintiest and neatest-growing of the gallicas.

■ ABOVE RIGHT

'DU MAITRE D'ECOLE'

A gallica rose that makes a compact plant
about 1m/3ft high and across, wider in
summer when the weight of blossom
makes the stems arch over. The fully
double, quartered-rosette, carmine-pink
flowers open flat and fade to lilac-pink and
grey. The dense, matt mid-green foliage is
abundant. The date of introduction of 'Du
Maître d'Ecole' is debated but is said by
some authorities to be 1840.

■ RIGHT

'DUC DE GUICHE'

A gallica rose that forms a shrub 1.2m/4ft
high and across. In summer it produces
large, fully double, highly scented, rich
crimson flowers; as they age, the petals
develop purple veining, the flowers finally
flushing purple. The leaves are matt dark
green. 'Duc de Guiche', an outstanding
gallica, is of uncertain origin and date.

R. GALLICA VAR. *OFFICINALIS*

(syn. *R. officinalis*)
A gallica rose, recorded in gardens since
the 13th century. It makes a bushy shrub
up to 1.2m/4ft high and across. In summer
it produces many large, semi-double,
sweetly fragrant, crimson flowers that open
flat to reveal golden stamens. The leaves
are coarse. *R. gallica* var. *officinalis* is a
superb garden plant that is rich in historical
associations as the red rose of Lancaster, the
medieval apothecary's rose and Provins rose.

'PRESIDENT DE SEZE'

**(syn. 'Jenny Duval', 'Madame
Hébert')**
A gallica rose, introduced before 1836, that
grows into a sturdy shrub 1.2m/4ft high by
1m/3ft across. In summer it produces
large, quartered, richly scented flowers; the
centre petals are rich magenta-purple, with
the colour fading across the flower to a soft
lilac-pink, which is almost white, at the
edges. The leaves are larger than is usual
for a gallica. A well-grown specimen of
'Président de Sèze' is a remarkable sight
when in full bloom.

■ LEFT

'TUSCANY SUPERB'

A gallica rose, raised before 1837, making an erect shrub 1.5m/5ft high and 1m/3ft across. The large, semi-double, lightly scented, deep crimson flowers, produced in mid-summer, open flat, showing golden stamens, then fade to purple. The foliage is abundant. Tolerant of poor soil, 'Tuscany Superb' may be used for hedging; it richly deserves its common name, double velvet rose.

■ LEFT

R. GALLICA 'VERSICOLOR'

A gallica rose, recorded in the 16th century but probably much older. It makes a neat shrub up to 1.2m/4ft high and across. The lightly scented flowers, produced in mid-summer, are semi-double, opening flat to reveal golden stamens. The petals are pale pink, splashed and striped with red and crimson. The leaves are dull mid-green. *R. gallica* 'Versicolor' is commonly known as *Rosa mundi*, after Fair Rosamund, the mistress of Henry II of England.

Other types

■ RIGHT

'BUFF BEAUTY'

This modern shrub rose, sometimes classified as a hybrid musk, was probably bred before 1939. It grows to about 1.5m/ 5ft high and across. The cupped, fully double, sweetly scented, pale buff-apricot flowers are carried in clusters in two flushes, the autumn flowering being less profuse. The leaves are tinged reddish-purple when young, turning dark green. 'Buff Beauty' can be used for hedging but, with the weight of the flowers on the canes, may need the support of horizontal wires. Mildew may be a problem.

■ LEFT

'FERGIE'

(syn. 'Ganfer')
A modern rose, usually classified as a cluster-flowered or patio rose, with a height and spread of 50cm/20in. From summer to autumn, it produces trusses of orange-buff flowers with pink-edged petals. The leaves are mid-green. 'Fergie' has much of the style of the old roses; the flowers are similar to those of 'Buff Beauty', but the plant is more compact.

■ RIGHT
'FRUHLINGSGOLD'

(syn. 'Spring Gold')
A pimpinellifolia hybrid, sometimes
classified as a modern shrub rose, it was
introduced in 1937. It makes a vigorous
shrub, each arching cane reaching up to
2.1m/7ft long. The large, cupped, semi-
double, fragrant, primrose-yellow flowers
cover the stems in late spring to early
summer. The flowers open flat from long,
pointed buds to display golden stamens.
The long, green leaves are pointed.
'Frühlingsgold' is a tough, thorny plant,
which is excellent planted as a barrier.

■ LEFT
'GRAHAM THOMAS'

(syn. 'Ausmas')
This modern shrub or 'English' rose,
which was raised in 1983, forms a vigorous
shrub 1.2–2.4m/4–8ft high with a similar
spread. The flowers, produced from
summer to autumn, are cupped, fully
double, fragrant and rich yellow. The
leaves are glossy. Named in honour of the
great English rosarian, Graham Stuart
Thomas, 'Graham Thomas' was considered
a notable introduction, since yellow is
virtually absent among true old roses.

■ RIGHT

'GRUSS AN AACHEN'

A polyantha rose, usually classified as a
cluster-flowered bush. It was bred around
1909 and makes a bush up to 1.5m/5ft
high and across. The shapely, deeply
cupped, fully double, delicately scented
flowers are tinged pink on opening then
fade to creamy white and are carried in
clusters from summer to autumn. The
leaves are dark green and leathery. Its long
flowering season and low habit of growth
make 'Gruss an Aachen' an outstanding
bedding rose.

■ RIGHT

'MANY HAPPY RETURNS'

(syn. 'Harwanted')
A modern rose, sometimes classified as
a cluster-flowered bush with a height
and spread of 75cm/2½ft. The shapely,
semi-double, lightly scented flowers are
blush-pink and appear from early
summer to autumn. The leaves are
glossy and dark green. With its long
flowering season, 'Many Happy Returns'
makes an excellent bedding rose.

■ *ABOVE*

'STANWELL PERPETUAL'

A pimpinellifolia hybrid, raised in 1838, which forms a dense, prickly shrub that can reach 1.5m/5ft high and across. The double, sweetly scented, blush-pink to white flowers that open flat are produced almost continuously throughout the summer. The leaves are grey-green. 'Stanwell Perpetual' tolerates poor soil and some shade, so it may be planted in woodland. It also makes a good hedge.

Modern
Roses

Introduction

Most modern roses combine a cast-iron constitution with an unrivalled length of flowering. Some are dainty and elegant, others are richly coloured show-stoppers. Many are deliciously fragrant. In addition to their value in beds and borders, modern roses can be used in other parts of the garden. Their value as ground cover should not be overlooked, while those with a neat, compact habit are ideal for growing in a container, either on the terrace or a patio. There are even modern roses that have been bred to provide long-lasting blooms for the flower arranger.

■ PREVIOUS PAGE
'Alpine Sunset' has richly scented
peach-pink flowers that shade to yellow.

■ RIGHT
Modern roses reward the gardener with
beautiful flowers throughout summer.

The history of the modern rose

The birth of the modern rose is usually held to have been in 1867 with 'La France'. Raised by Jean-Baptiste Guillot in France, this was considered an important novelty in rose breeding because it combined the long season and elegant flower shape of Chinese tea roses, from which it was descended, with the robust habit and hardiness of European roses.

'La France' was initially classified as a hybrid perpetual, a group of roses now more or less obsolete because they are leggy and difficult to place in the garden. It was soon realized, however, that this was a new type of rose, and the class hybrid tea was created. Today hybrid teas are officially, if rather less elegantly, known as large-flowered bush roses, although the name hybrid tea is still widely used.

Further selection and breeding refined the type, but the most significant breakthrough occurred early in the 20th century and involved the bright yellow *R. foetida*, which comes from central Asia but is confusingly known as the Austrian briar rose. The species has two forms, 'Bicolor' and 'Persiana'. 'Bicolor' (syn. 'Rose Capucine'), commonly known as the Austrian copper rose,

■ LEFT
The hybrid tea rose 'Remember Me' bears fully double, warm orange flowers from summer to autumn.

has vivid orange petals with a yellow reverse. 'Persiana' (syn. *R. foetida* var. *persiana*), which is known as the Persian yellow rose, has double yellow flowers. These were used to create an unprecedented colour range, including exciting bicolour and striped roses. The heyday of the old roses, with their somewhat restricted palette of white, pink and maroon, was over.

The new hybrid teas were bred with polyanthas – another largely obsolete rose group, which yields trusses of small flowers – to increase the flower size of the polyanthas. The

resulting roses were classified as hybrid polyanthas. Further breeding, notably in Britain, Denmark and the United States, produced roses with even larger flowers, although they were never as large as those of the hybrid teas.

'Rochester', which was introduced in 1934, was the first rose to be classified as a floribunda – that is, producing smallish flowers in large sprays – but although the term was widely used it never fully gained universal recognition. Other classifications included "floribunda hybrid tea-type" (plants with large

■ BELOW

The award-winning 'Dawn Chorus' was introduced in 1993. It is a vigorous, free flowering plant, ideal for rose beds.

flowers) and "grandiflora" (very tall roses), which meant that different terms were being used simultaneously for a range of roses that had certain broad similarities. Nowadays, all such roses are classified as cluster-flowered bush roses.

These two groups, the hybrid teas and the floribundas, gradually came to dominate the rose market, being easy to grow and reliable. They also had a long flowering season and proved ideal for bedding. Many are still planted *en masse* for bold displays of solid blocks of colour in public parks and gardens.

Towards the end of the 20th century, however, there was a renewed interest in cottage gardens and old roses enjoyed a renaissance. The mixed border, involving shrubs, perennials, annuals and bulbs, became the norm, and the prevailing style became increasingly relaxed. Many hybrid teas and floribundas were too stiff and uncompromising to fit easily into such schemes. Besides, some proved increasingly susceptible to disease and with the trend towards environmentally friendly forms of pest control, they fell out of favour with many gardeners.

Breeders turned their attention towards tough, hardy plants that have

a long season of interest and are disease resistant. Compact plants that smother themselves with flowers are now the ideal. Further hybridization produced several new classes. There are now roses for all manner of garden applications, including the so-called patio roses (strictly, dwarf cluster-flowered roses), ground-cover roses and miniatures. The recent trend towards smaller roses is

remarkable. Miniature varieties first appeared early in the 19th century, but were regarded as little more than novelties. Today they enjoy widespread appeal, and new varieties appear regularly.

Modern roses remain an enduring favourite, whatever the style of garden, rewarding their growers with a beautiful display of flowers right through the summer.

Modern roses in the garden

Such is the diversity of modern roses that their use in the garden is virtually unlimited. Whether you are looking for plants large or small, with strong or muted colours, rich perfume, a long flowering season or for growing in containers, there is a rose to answer to every need.

Bedding

For many gardeners the large- and cluster-flowered roses are synonymous with bedding. A uniform effect is best created by sticking to one variety. If you want to mix varieties, check the final heights

MODERN ROSES FOR BEDDING SCHEMES

'Alexander' (red)

'Allgold' (yellow)

'Chinatown' (golden-yellow)

'Elina' (creamy white)

'Just Joey' (orange)

'Sexy Rexy' (light clear pink)

'Super Star' (red)

and group the tallest at the back of the border or in the centre of an island bed, with shorter growing varieties in front. By planting miniatures at their feet you can create a bed that is roughly triangular in cross-section.

For maximum impact, use the luminous 'Super Star' (syn. 'Tanorstar', 'Tropicana'), or 'Precious Platinum' (syn. 'Opa Pötschke'), which are among the best of the reds. 'Allgold' is a good yellow, which keeps its colour well, while among the salmon-orange roses 'Anne Harkness' (syn. 'Harkaramel') and 'Amber Queen' (syn. 'Harroony', 'Prinz Eugen van Savoyen') are outstanding. Possibly even more eye-catching are those roses that combine two colours, such as 'Piccadilly' (syn. 'Macar')

■ RIGHT
The brilliant red flowers of 'Fred Loads' set alight a planting of herbaceous perennials.

(scarlet and yellow) and 'Circus' (whose flowers open yellow, mature to red, and fade to orange and pink).

For a more subtle approach, 'Iceberg' (syn. 'Korbin', 'Fée des Neiges', 'Schneewittchen'), 'Margaret Merril' (syn. 'Harkuly') and 'Pascali' (syn. 'Lenip') are some of the most rain-resistant whites. There are many excellent candidates among the pinks: 'Sexy Rexy' (syn. 'Heckenzauber', 'Macrexy') has a good clear colour, while 'The Queen Elizabeth', a deep cyclamen-pink, is one of the most versatile of all roses.

You can edge your rose bed with other bedding plants. Pelargoniums have a long flowering season and come in a similar colour range to roses, although there is no yellow. African and French marigolds (*Tagetes* cvs.) come in cheerful oranges and yellows, and attract the insects that prey on aphids. If you want to add a touch of blue, a colour that roses cannot provide, ageratum or lobelia are good choices.

Standards

Standard roses are not trained as such but are normal bush roses grafted on to stems of a vigorous species such as *Rosa rugosa*. They are available as full standards on a stem about 1.2m/4ft high or as half-standards, which are about 75cm/2½ft high. They produce a lollipop shape, although grafted

■ ABOVE
For a pot-pourri of summer scent, roses can be combined with annual tobacco plants (*Nicotiana* spp.).

ground-cover roses or climbers produce a weeping tree.

You can deploy standards in a formal scheme to striking effect. They can rise above a sea of bedding roses, either to contrast with or complement them, or they can be used in a small garden to line a path, creating a miniature, tree-lined avenue. Standards can also be used individually to mark the end of a vista or in a lawn, or in pairs at the start of a path or flight of steps. Standards in containers add style to a doorway. Remember, however, that they are bare in winter and should be replaced by evergreen hollies (*Ilex* spp.) or bays (*Laurus nobilis*).

■ LEFT
The cluster-flowered bush rose 'Eye Paint'
is planted *en masse* beneath the honey
locust, *Gleditsia triacanthos* 'Sunburst'.

rock gardens. Mulch well in the garden, preferably with bark chippings, not because they are greedier than other types of rose but to help suppress any weeds. Unlike other ground-cover plants, they do not always form weed-suppressing mats, and weeding through the thorny stems can be a thankless task.

Roses as ground cover

Mostly of recent introduction and increasingly popular, ground-cover roses generally have a compact, spreading habit, forming low, dome-shaped mounds. They look best in informal plantings.

Some are closely allied to rambling species that have a lax habit, and in some cases they have inherited their single flowers. These suit a wild garden, combining well with other flowers that have not been heavily hybridized, such as poppies (*Papaver* spp.) and species peonies, such as the Caucasian peony (*Paeonia mlokosewitschii*), which has lemon-yellow flowers. 'Nozomi' (syn. 'Heideröslein'), which was introduced in 1968 and has blush-white flowers, is one of the earliest of the type but is

still one of the best for this purpose. There are, however, many more recent introductions that are equally suitable. 'Red Meidiland' (syn. 'Meineble'), which has bright red flowers, is outstanding and has the advantage of conspicuous hips that redden in autumn.

Ground-cover roses can also be planted to cover banks or to cascade over the sides of raised beds. They are equally effective in containers or in

MODERN ROSES FOR HEDGING
'Alexander'
'Anne Harkness'
'Chinatown'
'Super Star'
'The Queen Elizabeth'

Other uses

Some modern roses can be planted as hedges. While they have an unrivalled flowering season among hedging plants, they do have the disadvantage of being deciduous and cannot provide a year-round barrier. Two fine varieties for the purpose are 'Chinatown' (syn. 'Ville de Chine'), which has golden-yellow flowers, and 'The Queen Elizabeth', with pink flowers. Both grow to 1.8m/6ft or more if lightly pruned. Other roses will form lower hedges, rugosas being especially effective with their tough, attractive foliage. Miniatures, such as 'Baby Masquerade' (syn. 'Tanba', 'Baby Carnival'), make an attractive low hedge or edging to a border.

Some modern roses also make highly effective lawn specimens. Again, 'Chinatown' is a very good candidate, but better still is 'Iceberg'.

■ BELOW
A pair of striking standard roses are used to mark an entrance.

Requiring only the minimum of pruning over a number of years, it will develop into an impressive shrub whose shape lives up to its name.

Roses with other plants

Mixed planting is now very popular, with all types of plants – shrubs, herbaceous perennials, bulbs and annuals – being grown together to make an informal scheme providing pleasure over a long season. Such a mix also attracts a wide range of beneficial insects. Roses are prime candidates for the mixed border, but are best kept at a distance from other greedy shrubs and trees, which may compete for moisture and nutrients.

Certain shrubs make dramatic backdrops. The dense, blackish-green of a yew hedge looks good with roses of any colour, but more adventurous gardeners might prefer the grey-green cider gum (*Eucalyptus gunnii*) or, more dramatically a purple-leaved form of *Berberis thunbergii* or *Cotinus coggygria*, which look sensational behind a vivid orange rose such as 'Whisky Mac' (syn. 'Tanky', 'Whisky'). Cut these shrubs back annually for the best foliage effect.

For an "old world" look, mix your roses with any of the traditional, cottage garden herbaceous plants. Lupins, Canterbury bells (*Campanula medium*) or foxgloves (*Digitalis* spp.) will provide strong verticals, while frothy, yellow-green lady's mantle (*Alchemilla mollis*) or bronze fennel (*Foeniculum vulgare* 'Purpureum') are marvellous fillers. In addition, try the larger, striking alliums with their spherical heads of almost geometric precision. For a more informal look in your garden, opt for Peruvian lilies (*Alstroemeria ligtu* hybrids) or day-lilies (*Hemerocallis* cvs.), both of which now have an extended range of cultivars in a variety of colours.

■ RIGHT
■ RIGHT
This scheme combines a large-flowered rose with *Geum* 'Mrs J. Bradshaw', *Lychnis chalcedonica* and *Valeriana officinalis*.

Because modern roses flower for several months, you will need to accompany them with a few late-flowering perennials, such as anemones, crocosmias and cannas. Some tender perennials have a comparably long flowering season, notably osteospermums and the blue daisy (*Felicia amelloides*). Half-hardy annuals, such as tobacco plants (*Nicotiana* spp.), also combine well with roses, as does the Texan bluebell (*Eustoma grandiflorum*).

For a jungle-like effect allow a late-flowering clematis – a texensis or

■ BELOW
The profusion of large flower clusters in this massed planting of 'Iceberg' looks effective against the pinks (*Dianthus*) and hardy geraniums.

viticella type such as 'Gravetye Beauty' (crimson red) or 'Minuet' (white) – to wander through neighbouring plants. Cut back hard annually when you prune the roses.

For a vibrant colour scheme mix the rich amber-yellow 'Glenfiddich' or the rich vermilion 'Alexander' with a red-hot poker, such as the orange-red *Kniphofia* 'Prince Igor', and the aptly named bright-red *Crocosmia* 'Lucifer'. *Hemerocallis* 'Scarlet Orbit' could complete the picture, with annual orange nasturtiums at their feet. You can easily tone down this lively colour scheme with grey-leaved lambs' ears (*Stachys byzantina*; syn. *S. olympica*), the grey curry plant (*Helichrysum italicum* subsp. *serotinum*) or one of the artemisias.

For an altogether gentler scheme try the queen of foliage plants, the hosta. Roses with pink in the

■ RIGHT
The neat bushes of 'Amber Queen' have
been planted to echo the shape of the
classical columns.

■ RIGHT
The neat bushes of 'Amber Queen' have
been planted to echo the shape of the
classical columns.

colouring look best with glaucous
hostas, such as *H. sieboldiana* var.
elegans or 'Frances Williams', while
the yellows and reds mix well with
the brighter 'Sum and Substance' or
'August Moon'. Subtly coloured
carnations and pinks (*Dianthus* spp.)
also blend well with roses and have
the advantage of attractive foliage.

There are many excellent modern
roses for the scented garden. Create
an even richer fragrance by stirring in
the delicious regal lily (*Lilium regale*),
or sweet peas (*Lathyrus odoratus*). A
mock orange (*Philadelphus* spp.) will
make a glorious scented background.

MODERN ROSES GROWN FOR THEIR SCENT

'Alec's Red'	'Fragrant Cloud'
'Alexander'	'Helen Traubel'
'Apricot Nectar'	'Ingrid Bergman'
'Arthur Bell'	'Josephine Bruce'
'Betty Prior'	'Lady Hillingdon'
'Blue Moon'	'Margaret Merril'
'Bobby Charlton'	'Mister Lincoln'
'Crimson Glory'	'Red Devil'
'Double Delight'	'Royal William'
'Dutch Gold'	'Sheila's Perfume'
'Elizabeth Harkness'	'Sutter's Gold'
'English Miss'	'Whisky Mac'
'Escapade'	'Yesterday'

Roses in containers

With the trend towards ever smaller
gardens, rose breeders have turned
their attention to producing dwarf,
more compact roses that can be
grown in containers. Some are no
more than 30cm/1ft high. You can
grow them individually or make the
rose the centrepiece of a large
container, surrounding it with ivies
(*Hedera* spp.), trailing lobelia or the
tender orange-red to scarlet parrot's
beak (*Lotus berthelotti*). The tiniest
roses can be planted in hanging
baskets – those with trailing stems
being particularly effective.

Plant Catalogue

Roses are arranged according to the following categories:

Cluster-flowered (floribunda)
Large-flowered (hybrid tea)
Rugosa

The height and spread listed in the descriptions are those that the rose can be expected to achieve on maturity. They will vary, of course, depending on season, climate and soil type.

■ RIGHT
'AMBER QUEEN'

(syn. 'Harroony', 'Prinz Eugen van Savoyen')
A cluster-flowered (floribunda) bush rose of neat habit, introduced in 1984, which will attain a height of 80cm/32in and a spread of 65cm/26in. In summer and autumn it produces clusters of fully double, heavily scented, rich amber-yellow flowers, which open from rounded buds. The leaves are tinged red on emergence. Good for bedding, hedges and containers.

■ RIGHT
'ANNE BOLEYN'

Named after Henry VIII's unhappy second queen, this rose, bred by David Austin, shows exceptional disease resistance. The soft warm pink flowers are generously produced over a long period in summer and into autumn. The leaves are glossy light green. It is fairly robust, growing to 1.2m/4ft with a similar spread.

Cluster-flowered (floribunda) roses

■ RIGHT
'ANNE HARKNESS'
(syn. 'Harkaramel')

A cluster-flowered (floribunda) bush rose
of upright, branching habit, introduced in
1980. It will grow to about 1.2m/4ft high
and 60cm/2ft across. The pointed, urn-
shaped, double, soft buff-yellow flowers are
borne in large clusters from late summer to
autumn. The leaves are mid-green.
Spectacular in full flower, 'Anne Harkness'
is a disease-resistant rose that is suitable for
bedding, hedging and cutting.

■ BELOW
'ARTHUR BELL'

A cluster-flowered (floribunda) bush rose of
upright, branching habit, introduced in
1965. It will achieve a height of 1m/3ft and
a spread of 60cm/2ft. From summer to
autumn it produces clusters of semi-double
to double, strongly scented, bright yellow
flowers that pale as they age. The leaves are
leathery and glossy. 'Arthur Bell' is a versatile
rose; the autumn flowering is especially good.

■ FAR LEFT
'CHINATOWN'

(syn. 'Ville de Chine')
A cluster-flowered (floribunda) bush rose of bushy, upright habit, introduced in 1963, which grows to 1.5m/5ft high and 1m/3ft across. Clusters of fully double, fragrant, bright golden-yellow flowers are freely produced throughout the summer into autumn. The leaves are glossy dark green. One of the largest of its type, 'Chinatown' can be grown at the back of a border, as a hedge or as a specimen.

■ ABOVE RIGHT
'ELIZABETH OF GLAMIS'

(syn. 'Irish Beauty', 'Macel')
A cluster-flowered (floribunda) bush rose of upright habit, introduced in 1964. It grows to 75cm/2½ft high and 60cm/2ft across. Clusters of double, sweetly scented, salmon-pink flowers are carried throughout the summer and autumn. The leaves are dark green and semi-glossy. 'Elizabeth of Glamis' is an outstanding rose of its type and has stood the test of time. It does not always thrive on cold, heavy soils but is lovely when grown in the right conditions.

■ LEFT
'DARCEY BUSSELL'

With its short, bushy growth, to about 1m/3ft by 60cm/2ft, this rose would be an excellent choice for growing in a container. The rich crimson flowers, have a moderate, fruity fragrance. The colour will fade to mauve as the petals fall. They are produced in succession over a long period in summer. The leaves are mid-green.

ABOVE
ESCAPADE'

(syn. 'Harpade')
A cluster-flowered (floribunda) bush rose of freely branching habit,
ntroduced in 1967, which grows to 1.2m/4ft high and 60cm/2ft
across. The semi-double, sweetly scented flowers are of unique
colouring: borne in clusters from summer to autumn, they are soft
ilac-pink, opening flat to reveal white centres and golden stamens.
It occasionally produces pure white flowers within the cluster. The
eaves are glossy bright green. A good disease-resistant rose.

■ ABOVE
'DRUMMER BOY'

(syn. 'Harvacity')
A cluster-flowered (floribunda) rose of
spreading habit introduced in 1987. The
dense clusters of many small, semi-
double flowers with fimbriated (frilled)
petals are produced in profusion
throughout summer. Although virtually
scentless, the flowers are an eye-catching
deep red. 'Drummer Boy' has a height
and spread of 50cm/20in, and makes an
excellent choice for a container or as low
edging at the front of a border.

■ LEFT
'EYE PAINT'

(syn. 'Maceye', 'Tapis Persan')
A cluster-flowered (floribunda) bush or shrub rose, with a free-
branching habit, introduced in 1975. It will grow to 1.2m/4ft high
and 75cm/2½ft across. Large clusters of single, lightly scented
flowers cover the bush in summer and autumn; bright scarlet, they
open flat to reveal white centres and golden stamens. 'Eye Paint'
does best with light pruning and makes a good hedge. Deadhead
regularly to maintain the flowering performance.

■ RIGHT

'GOLDEN WEDDING'

(syn. 'Arokris')

A cluster-flowered (floribunda) rose which will grow to 80cm/32in high and 60cm/2ft across. It carries trusses of double, luminous yellow flowers over a long period from summer to autumn. With its sumptuous blooms, 'Golden Wedding' is sometimes classified as a large-flowered rose.

■ LEFT

'FRED LOADS'

A cluster-flowered (floribunda) rose growing to a height of 2m/6½ft with a spread of 1m/3ft. It produces a succession of brilliant red, semi-double flowers from summer to autumn. A tall-growing rose, 'Fred Loads' is an excellent candidate for the back of a border.

■ LEFT
'HARVEST FAYRE'

(syn. 'Dicnorth')
A cluster-flowered (floribunda) rose
which grows to 75cm/2½ft high with a
spread of about 60cm/2ft. The dainty,
tea-like, soft yellowish-orange flowers
have a pleasing scent and are carried
amid glossy green leaves. The flowering
display continues until late autumn,
hence the name.

■ RIGHT
'HANNAH GORDON'

(syn. 'Korweiso', 'Raspberry Ice')
A cluster-flowered (floribunda) bush rose of spreading, open habit,
introduced in 1983. It will grow to 80cm/32in high and
65cm/26in across. In summer and autumn it produces clusters of
lightly scented, double flowers that have creamy pink petals
shading to deeper pink at the edges. The leaves are glossy dark
green. A disease-resistant rose, 'Hannah Gordon' is good for
cutting and can also be grown in a container.

■ RIGHT
'ICEBERG'

(syn. 'Korbin', 'Fée des Neiges', 'Schneewittchen')

A cluster-flowered (floribunda) bush rose of elegant, branching habit, introduced in 1958. It achieves a height of 1.5m/5ft and a spread of 1m/3ft. From summer to autumn abundant clusters of double, ivory-white, lightly scented flowers open from tapering, pink-flushed buds. The leaves are glossy bright green. An outstanding rose, 'Iceberg' can be used for bedding, hedging, cutting or, with minimum pruning, as a specimen.

■ LEFT
'KORRESIA'

(syn. 'Friesia', 'Sunsprite')

A cluster-flowered (floribunda) bush rose of neat, upright habit, introduced in 1974. It grows to 75cm/2½ft high and 60cm/2ft across. From summer to autumn clusters of shapely buds open to double, fragrant, bright golden-yellow flowers that hold their colour well. The leaves are glossy light green. 'Korresia' can be used for bedding and to provide cut flowers.

■ ABOVE LEFT

'LILLI MARLENE'

(syn. 'Korlima')

A cluster-flowered (floribunda) bush rose
of slender, branching habit, introduced in
1959, which grows to 70cm/28in high and
60cm/2ft across. Large clusters of double,
lightly scented, rich crimson flowers are
produced from summer to autumn on
plum red shoots. The leaves are dark green,
tinted red on emergence. 'Lilli Marlene' is
tolerant of both rain and hot sun.

■ ABOVE RIGHT

'L'AIMANT'

This delightful variety, with bushy,
compact growth to a height and spread of
no more than 1m/3ft, freely produces its
fully double, soft coral pink flowers over
a long period in summer to autumn.
A strong fragrance from the flowers adds
to the charms of this particular variety.
The foliage benefits from showing
excellent disease resistance.

■ ABOVE

'MARGARET MERRIL'

(syn. 'Harkuly')

A cluster-flowered (floribunda) bush rose of upright habit, introduced in 1977, which
grows to 1m/3ft high and 60cm/2ft across. Clusters of large, shapely, double, sweetly
scented, pure-white flowers are carried from summer to autumn. The leaves are glossy dark
green. Besides its versatility in the garden, 'Margaret Merril' can also be grown in
containers and used as a cut flower. Blackspot can be a problem.

■ ABOVE LEFT
'MOUNTBATTEN'

(syn. 'Harmantelle')
A cluster-flowered (floribunda) bush rose of dense, upright habit, introduced in 1982, which grows to 1.5m/5ft high and 1m/3ft across. Small clusters of large, double, lightly scented, yellow flowers are carried from summer to autumn. The leaves are glossy dark green. An excellent specimen, needing only minimum pruning.

■ ABOVE RIGHT
'SHEILA'S PERFUME'

(syn. 'Harsherry')
A cluster-flowered (floribunda) bush rose of upright habit, introduced in 1985. It grows to 75cm/2½ft high and 60cm/2ft across. The flowers, carried singly and in clusters from summer to autumn, are double and sweetly scented; the petals are yellow marked with red, fading to pink. The leaves are glossy dark green. 'Sheila's Perfume' makes an excellent low hedge, grows well in containers and provides good cut flowers.

■ LEFT
'SEXY REXY'

(syn. 'Macrexy', 'Heckenzauber')
A cluster-flowered (floribunda) bush rose of upright habit, introduced in 1984. It has a height and spread of 60cm/2ft. Clusters of shapely, fully double, lightly scented, clear light-pink flowers are produced in summer and autumn. The leaves are glossy dark green. A versatile rose, good in containers and as a cut flower.

■ ABOVE
'THE TIMES ROSE'

This excellent bedding rose produces a blaze of crimson red flowers, held in large clusters among dark green leaves, throughout summer. The fragrance is only light. Height and spread to 1m/3ft. 'The Times Rose' was bred by the German rose grower Kordes.

■ ABOVE
'THE QUEEN ELIZABETH'

(syn. 'Queen Elizabeth')
A cluster-flowered (floribunda) bush rose of strongly upright habit, introduced in 1954. It will grow to 2.1m/7ft or more high and 1m/3ft across. From summer to autumn it produces clusters of large, fully double, only lightly scented, china-pink flowers. The leaves are glossy dark green. A good rose for the back of a border or as a hedge. The flowers last well when cut.

■ RIGHT
'YESTERDAY'

(syn. 'Tapis d'Orient')
A polyantha or cluster-flowered (floribunda) shrub rose of elegant, open, spreading habit, introduced in 1974, and achieving a height and spread of 1m/3ft or more. From summer to autumn clusters of semi-double, fragrant, deep lilac-pink flowers, produced in succession, open flat to reveal paler centres and golden stamens. The leaves are glossy dark green. It has any number of uses in the garden and provides good cut flowers. With minimum pruning, it makes an attractive specimen.

■ ABOVE LEFT
'BLUE MOON'

(syn. 'Blue Monday', 'Mainzer Fastnacht', 'Sissi',
'Tannacht')
A large-flowered (hybrid tea) bush rose of upright, branching habit,
introduced in 1964, which will grow to 1m/3ft high and 60cm/2ft
across. In summer and autumn shapely, fully double, silvery-lilac
flowers that are sweetly scented are carried in abundance. The
leaves are large and dark green. Generally considered to be the best
blue rose, 'Blue Moon' needs careful placing in the garden because
of its curious colouring. It is perhaps best grown under glass.

■ ABOVE RIGHT
'BOBBY CHARLTON'

A large-flowered (hybrid tea) rose of upright habit, introduced in
1974. It will grow to 1m/3ft high and 60cm/2ft across. It produces
high-centred, fully double, scented, soft-pink flowers from late
summer to autumn. The large leaves are dark green and semi-
glossy. Generally a healthy rose, 'Bobby Charlton' performs well in
wet weather and is a good choice for exhibition.

■ RIGHT
'CHRYSLER IMPERIAL'

A large-flowered (hybrid tea) bush rose of neat, upright habit, introduced in 1952, which will grow to 1m/3ft high and 60cm/2ft across. The very fragrant, fully double, vivid red flowers open from pointed buds then fade to dull purplish-red. The leaves are dark green. 'Chrysler Imperial' is grown exclusively for the perfection of individual flowers and is a good rose for exhibition if disbudded. It is susceptible to disease.

■ BELOW RIGHT
'DOUBLE DELIGHT'

(syn. 'Andeli')

A large-flowered (hybrid tea) bush rose of freely branching habit, introduced in 1977. It will grow to 1m/3ft high and 60cm/2ft across. From summer to autumn it bears large, shapely, fully double, sweetly scented flowers that have creamy white petals flushed cherry-red at the edges. The leaves are semi-glossy. 'Double Delight' is an outstanding rose for bedding and cutting, though the flowers can be spoilt by rain.

■ OPPOSITE BELOW
'CHICAGO PEACE'

(syn. 'Johnago')

A large-flowered (hybrid tea) rose of bushy, spreading habit, introduced in 1962. It grows to 1.5m/5ft high and 1m/3ft across. The huge, only lightly scented flowers, produced from summer to autumn, have coppery pink petals with a yellow reverse. The leaves are glossy dark green. 'Chicago Peace', a sport of 'Peace', can be used as a specimen if pruned lightly; otherwise, use it for bedding or hedging.

■ RIGHT
'OLYMPIAD'

(syn. 'Macauck')
A large-flowered
(hybrid tea) rose of
upright, bushy
habit, introduced
in 1984. It will
grow to 1.2m/4ft
high and 60cm/2ft
across. The fully
double, only
lightly scented,
bright red flowers
are produced from
summer to
autumn. The
leaves are matt
mid-green.
'Olympiad' is
an excellent rose
for cutting.

■ BELOW LEFT
'PAPA MEILLAND'

(syn. 'Meisar')
A large-flowered (hybrid tea) bush rose of
upright habit, introduced in 1963. It will
grow to 1m/3ft high and 60cm/2ft across.
From summer to autumn it produces
shapely, fully double, fragrant, deep
crimson flowers. The leaves are glossy dark
green. 'Papa Meilland' is excellent as a cut
flower, although the flowering is not
profuse and it is prone to disease.

■ BELOW RIGHT
'PASCALI'

(syn. 'Lenip')
A large-flowered (hybrid tea) bush rose of
upright, open habit, introduced in 1963,
which will grow to 1m/3ft high and
75cm/2½ft across. Throughout summer
and autumn it produces shapely, double,
only lightly scented flowers that have white
petals shaded creamy buff. The leaves are
glossy dark green, but sparse. The flowers
of 'Pascali' show unsurpassed rain-
resistance; they are exceptionally long-
lasting when cut.

■ RIGHT

'PAUL SHIRVILLE'

(syn. 'Harqueterwife', 'Heart Throb')
A large-flowered (hybrid tea) rose of slightly spreading habit, introduced in 1983. It will grow to 1m/3ft high and 75cm/2½ft across. The double, fragrant, warm pink flowers are carried from summer to autumn. The leaves are large and dark green. 'Paul Shirville' tolerates poor soil and is good for bedding and containers.

■ LEFT

'PEACE'

(syn. 'Gioia', 'Gloria Dei', 'Mme A. Meilland')
A large-flowered (hybrid tea) bush rose of spreading, bushy habit, bred in 1942, which will grow to 1.2m/4ft or more high and 1m/3ft across. The large, fully double, only lightly scented flowers are pale yellow with pink flushes, and appear from mid-summer to autumn. The leaves are glossy dark green. One of the most popular and best known roses ever bred, 'Peace' is a vigorous plant, which makes a fine specimen with light pruning.

'ROYAL WILLIAM'

(syn. 'Duftzauber '84', 'Fragrant Charm '84', 'Korzaun')
A large-flowered (hybrid tea) rose of vigorous upright habit, introduced in 1984. It will grow to 1m/3ft high and 75cm/2½ft across. From summer to autumn it carries large, fully double, fragrant, deep red flowers on long stems. The leaves are glossy dark green. 'Royal William' is good for bedding and cutting.

■ BELOW
'RED DEVIL'

(syn. 'Dicam', 'Coeur d'Amour')
A large-flowered (hybrid tea) rose of bushy habit, introduced in 1967. It grows to 1m/3ft high and 75cm/2½ft across. From summer to autumn it produces large, shapely, fully double, fragrant, vivid scarlet flowers. The leaves are glossy dark green. 'Red Devil' is a good bedding rose, though the flowers can be spoilt by rain.

■ ABOVE
'PICCADILLY'

(syn. 'Macar')
A large-flowered (hybrid tea) bush rose of upright, branching habit, introduced in 1959. It grows to 1m/3ft or more high and 60cm/2ft across. From summer to autumn it produces double, only lightly scented flowers with bright scarlet petals with a yellow reverse ageing to orange. The leaves are glossy dark green, tinged bronze. 'Piccadilly' performs best in cool weather, bright sunlight turning the colour a more uniform orange. Blackspot can be a problem.

■ BELOW LEFT
'SAVOY HOTEL'

(syn. 'Harvintage', 'Integrity')
A large-flowered (hybrid tea) bush rose, introduced in 1989, which will grow to 1m/3ft high and 60cm/2ft across. From summer to autumn strong stems carry large, shapely, fully double, fragrant, clear-pink flowers. The leaves are dark green. 'Savoy Hotel' is a versatile rose that provides excellent material for cutting.

■ BELOW RIGHT
'SUPER STAR'

(syn. 'Tanorstar', 'Tropicana')
A large-flowered (hybrid tea) bush rose of branching but uneven habit, introduced in 1960. It will grow to 1m/3ft high and across. The large, shapely, double, lightly scented, luminous vermilion flowers are produced from summer to autumn. The leaves are semi-glossy. 'Super Star' is grown for the beauty of the individual blooms, but is susceptible to mildew.

■ BELOW
'WHISKY MAC'

(syn. 'Tanky', 'Whisky')
A large-flowered (hybrid tea) bush rose of upright habit, introduced in 1967. It will grow to 75cm/2½ft high and 60cm/2ft across. From summer to autumn it produces an abundance of large, fully double, strongly fragrant, rich amber-yellow flowers. The leaves are glossy dark green. Despite sometimes suffering from dieback and fungal diseases, 'Whisky Mac' retains its popularity because of its unique flower colour.

■ ABOVE
'WILLIAM SHAKESPEARE 2000'

This superb variety produces exquisite blooms of the richest velvety crimson, gradually changing to an equally rich purple. Deeply cupped at first, the flower soon opens out to a shallow quartered cup. The growth is neat and upright and the flowers have a warm scent. The bush grows to 100cm/36in by 80cm/32in. The variety also has excellent disease resistance.

Rugosa roses

■ RIGHT
'HANSA'

A rugosa rose of dense habit, introduced in 1905. It will grow to 1.2m/4ft high and 1m/3ft across. Double, very fragrant, reddish-purple flowers are freely produced throughout the summer; in autumn, large red hips develop. The leaves are wrinkled and dark green. A versatile rose, 'Hansa' can be grown in light shade.

■ ABOVE
'SCHNEEZWERG'

(syn. 'Snow Dwarf')
A rugosa rose of dense, spreading habit, introduced in 1912, which will grow to 1.2m/4ft high and 1.5m/5ft across. From late spring until late autumn it produces anemone-like, semi-double, only lightly scented, white flowers that open flat to reveal golden stamens; small orange-red hips follow. The leaves are greyish-green. The autumn display is particularly good; although the foliage does not change colour, flowers continue to appear alongside the reddening hips. For the best fruiting, deadhead selectively in summer.

■ ABOVE
'ROSERAIE DE L'HAY'

A rugosa rose of dense, vigorous, spreading habit, introduced in 1901. It will grow to at least 1.8m/6ft high and 1.2m/4ft across. Throughout the summer and into autumn it produces double, strongly scented, wine-red flowers that open to reveal creamy stamens. The wrinkled leaves redden in autumn. 'Roseraie de l'Haÿ' makes an excellent hedge and can also be planted in light shade.

Climbing Roses

The history of climbing roses

Climbing roses are a disparate group of plants that share no common ancestor. The term "climbing rose" is generally understood to include rambling roses, which usually have large trusses of small flowers produced in a single flush in mid-summer, as well as true climbing roses, which tend to flower recurrently. Ramblers generally produce masses of very flexible canes and flower on year-old wood. Climbers, which are often more stiffly upright, flower on new wood.

In the wild, few roses are natural climbers, but there are several that make huge, scrambling shrubs with long, flexible stems that are described botanically as scandent (ascending or loosely climbing). Such roses rapidly colonize any shrub or tree that impedes their progress by attaching themselves to the host plants by means of their sharp, hooked thorns.

Many climbing roses grown in gardens today have the Chinese species *Rosa gigantea* in their ancestry. As its name suggests, this is an enormous plant, which can reach a height and spread of 16.5m/54ft or more. Fortunately, most modern climbing roses are more restrained. Many rambling roses have been derived from *R. wichurana* (syn. *R. wichuraiana*), the memorial rose, a species found in Japan, Korea, China and Taiwan. It has lax stems that either trail or climb. The evergreen European *R. sempervirens* has also played a part, as has the Japanese *R. multiflora*.

Some climbing roses are sports (spontaneous mutations) of bush roses. A climbing sport can be recognized by having "Climbing" in its name – for example, 'Climbing Cécile Brünner' or 'Climbing The Queen Elizabeth'.

Some of the old-fashioned
Bourbon roses, such as 'Louise Odier'
and 'Madame Isaac Pereire', both of
which have long, flexible stems, can
also be grown as climbers, as can
some of the China roses.

Although roses have been popular
garden plants for centuries, interest in
the breeding of new varieties of
climbing rose declined between the
two world wars. This lack of
popularity was possibly due to the
climbing rose's need for regular
maintenance – a neglected climber
can become a menace, making
impenetrable thickets of tough,
thorny stems – and the fact that
many flowered only once. As a result,
with a few exceptions, most of the
climbing roses grown in gardens
today were bred after 1949. The two
rose breeders who did most to revive
interest in breeding climbing roses
were Sam McGredy in Britain and

■ OPPOSITE

The magnificent 'Climbing Iceberg' is a good choice for clothing a wall, where its flowers look most graceful.

■ BELOW

'Albertine', one of the best-loved rambling roses of all time, at the height of its glory in mid-summer.

Wilhelm Kordes in Germany. Both concentrated on shorter growing varieties that were easier to manage. Breeders in the United States also made an important contribution, especially Dr Walter Van Fleet, who developed roses that could survive a cold North American winter. He bred the pink climber that bears his name, although today its repeat-flowering sport, 'New Dawn', has superseded it.

More recently a number of 'miniature' climbers have been introduced. These have small flowers and grow no more than 2.1m/7ft. They are ideal for the smaller garden or for growing in containers.

Climbing roses in the garden

There are few more idyllic images than that of a country cottage in high summer, with roses arching over the gate and covering the walls of the house. Town-dwellers can re-create this effect too. A climbing rose will lend an air of timelessness and maturity, even to the most modern home. Choose one of the heavily scented varieties, such as 'Albertine', 'New Dawn' or 'Zéphirine Drouhin'. Their scent will be especially appreciated near an open window. 'Zéphirine Drouhin' is particularly well suited for growing around a door because it has no thorns to catch on the clothing of passers-by.

Climbing roses have a number of other uses in the garden. Where there is space, you could allow the rose to grow with the minimum of pruning

CLIMBING ROSES VALUED FOR THEIR SCENT

'Breath of Life'

'Climbing Ena Harkness'

'Climbing Etoile de Hollande'

'Climbing Lady Hillingdon'

'Compassion'

'Gloire de Dijon'

'Guinée'

'Leaping Salmon'

'Madame Alfred Carrière'

'Madame Grégoire Staechelin'

'Maigold'

'Mermaid'

'New Dawn'

'Paul's Lemon Pillar'

'Rosy Mantle'

'Schoolgirl'

'Zéphirine Drouhin'

■ LEFT
Roses scrambling over an archway are quintessential ingredients of a country garden. As well as bringing a delightful froth of blooms high above the path, the archway creates a simple screening effect that offers an illusion of space.

■ BELOW
A climbing rose trained along a rope in a catenary or curve looks delightful.

■ BELOW
Clematis 'The President' makes a sensational clash with the brilliant scarlet 'Danse du Feu'.

to produce a huge fountain of flowers. The rambling 'Albertine', grown in this way, makes a magnificent 6m/20ft high shrub and is one of the glories of the mid-summer garden.

'Albertine' and some other ramblers are available as weeping standards, grafted on to 1.2–1.8m/ 4–6ft stems of *R. canina* or *R. rugosa*, so that you can create a cascade of flowers even in a confined area.

Climbing roses also look stunning grown over pergolas. Rustic poles are appropriate in cottage gardens, although brick pillars linked by wooden beams may last longer.

You can also train roses on ropes slung between two uprights to create garlands of flowers, called a catenary, at the back of a border. For this purpose choose a medium-growing variety with long, flexible stems, such as 'Madame Grégoire Staechelin' (syn. 'Spanish Beauty'), which can be looped around the rope to produce festoons of flowers. Shorter-growing types, such as 'Handel' (syn. 'Macha'), or one of the Bourbon roses, such as 'Madame Isaac Pereire' or 'Louise Odier' (syn. 'L'Ouche', 'Madame de Stella'), can be planted in the border and trained against pillars or tripods. Another possibility is to erect free-standing trellis panels. Train the roses against these to make a barrier that will be covered in flowers in summer but open in winter.

Rampant roses that grow up to and over 12m/40ft high are best accommodated in most gardens by allowing them to scramble through

■ LEFT
A climbing or rambling rose can make a spectacular impression if grown up a tree.

■ BELOW
The banana-scented 'Seagull' wings its way through a large mature conifer.

trees, but take care to choose a suitably robust host plant that will be able to take the weight of the fully grown rose. Large conifers planted principally for winter interest are good candidates. An old orchard of apple or cherry trees would look enchanting wreathed in climbing roses flowering amongst the branches. Although this is a spectacular way of growing vigorous roses such as 'Climbing Cécile Brünner', 'Seagull' or 'Albéric Barbier', bear in mind that the rose must be matched to the size of the tree. A large vigorous rambler will very soon smother a small tree, eventually leading to its death.

Climbing roses can also be grown effectively by allowing them to ramble through shrubs, such as lilacs, which are dull after their show of flowers in late spring. This is a form of wild gardening, since a strict pruning regime in such a situation would be impractical.

You can trail a climbing rose up and over a wall to make a curtain of flowers on the other side. If you have a high garden wall, try pinning to it one of the more vigorous climbing roses, such as 'Paul's Lemon Pillar' (syn. 'Lemon Pillar'). If the wall is in the sun for much of the day select one of the roses that benefit from additional heat, such as 'Gloire de Dijon', the old glory rose, or a slightly tender China rose, such as *R. × odorata* 'Mutabilis'.

Climbing roses combine particularly well with other climbers, such as clematis or passion flowers (*Passiflora* spp.). You can create some

■ BELOW
Rich purple foxgloves provide the perfect contrast to white roses.

enchanting colour combinations if the plants flower at the same time, or you can choose an accompanying climber that flowers before or after the rose to extend the season of interest. For instance, the rose could support an earlier flowering macropetala clematis or a large-flowered clematis, such as 'The President', which would flower at the same time as the rose.

Team light colours with dark ones, combine complementaries or use shades of the same colour. The pale pink climbing rose 'New Dawn' would work equally well with the pink clematis 'Nelly Moser' or the deep purple 'Jackmanii'. Try the rich red climber 'Guinée' with the smoky pink clematis *C. viticella* 'Purpurea Plena Elegans' or 'Golden Showers' with the rich violet clematis 'Haku-ôkan'. In a white garden try the old climber 'Madame Alfred Carrière', which has a long flowering season and tolerates some shade, with the clematis 'Henryi'. Use white foxgloves (*Digitalis purpurea* f. *albiflora*) to provide vertical interest.

All climbing roses tend to become bare at the base in time. Mask this by underplanting with shallow-rooting perennials such as catmint (*Nepeta* spp.), lambs' ears (*Stachys byzantina*; syn. *S. olympica*), hostas or lady's mantle (*Alchemilla mollis*).

If you are restricted for space and have no more than a small patio or roof garden, or even just a balcony, you can still enjoy climbing roses by choosing from one of the miniature climbers, such as 'Nice Day', which are easily grown in a large container such as a half-barrel.

■ LEFT

'BOBBIE
JAMES'

A vigorous
rambling rose,
introduced in
1961, which will
grow to 10m/30ft
high and 6m/20ft
across. In summer
it covers itself with
clusters of small,
white, semi-
double flowers
that are sweetly
scented. The
leaves are glossy
green. 'Bobbie
James' is an
excellent choice
for growing into a
large tree.
Otherwise use
only where space
permits.

■ RIGHT

'RAMBLING RECTOR'

A vigorous rambling rose, introduced
before 1912, which will grow to 6m/20ft
high and across. In summer it covers itself
with clusters of small, single, white,
fragrant flowers; small red hips follow in
autumn. The leaves are glossy bright green.
'Rambling Rector', an impressive sight in
maturity when in full flower, is suitable for
growing into a large tree.

■ ABOVE AND INSET
'SEAGULL'

A rambling rose, introduced in 1907, which will grow to 6m/20ft high and 4m/13ft across. In summer it produces a single flush of clusters of small, white, single to semi-double, fragrant flowers. The leaves are greyish-green. Less vigorous than some other similar roses, 'Seagull' can be grown into a small to medium-sized tree.

■ RIGHT
'VEILCHENBLAU'

(syn. 'Blue Rambler', 'Violet Blue')
A vigorous rambling rose, introduced in 1909, which will grow to 4m/13ft high and across. In mid-summer it produces clusters of sweetly scented, semi-double, violet-pink flowers with yellow stamens. The flowers fade to purplish grey. The leaves are glossy and light green. More modest than most ramblers, 'Veilchenblau' is suitable for a small garden. It is best grown where there is some shelter from the mid-day sun.

Large climbers

■ BELOW

R. BANKSIAE 'LUTEA'

A vigorous climbing rose with a height and spread of 10m/30ft. Arching stems carry clusters of small, scentless, soft yellow flowers in a single crop in early summer. The leaves are small and pointed. Although it is fully hardy, *R. banksiae* 'Lutea' needs a sheltered spot, ideally against a warm wall, if it is to flower reliably. Mildew is sometimes a problem in late summer.

■ ABOVE

'CLIMBING CECILE BRUNNER'

A vigorous climbing rose, introduced in 1894, which will grow to 6m/20ft high and across. Over a long period in summer, large clusters of small, fully double, sweetly scented, pale pink flowers open from pointed buds. The leaves are plentiful. 'Climbing Cécile Brünner', a sport of the dainty China rose 'Cécile Brünner', is a good choice for growing through a tree; in other situations it can disappoint, since flowering is not always profuse.

■ LEFT

'MADAME GREGOIRE STAECHELIN'

(syn. 'Spanish Beauty')
A vigorous climbing rose, introduced in 1927. It will grow to 6m/20ft high and 4m/13ft across. In early summer fully double, rounded, sweetly scented, warm-pink flowers with slightly frilled petals are borne in profusion in hanging clusters. The leaves are matt green. 'Madame Grégoire Staechelin' flowers once only, but at its peak it can be sumptuous; it has large, showy hips that redden in autumn.

■ RIGHT

'MERMAID'

A vigorous climbing rose, introduced in 1918. It will grow to 6m/20ft high and across. From mid-summer until autumn single, pale yellow, fragrant flowers open from pointed buds to reveal prominent golden stamens that persist after the petals have fallen. The leaves are glossy and semi-evergreen or evergreen, depending on the season; the stems are viciously thorny. 'Mermaid' tolerates some shade and is best grown where it gets shelter from hard frosts. Although the flowers are not abundant, they are beautiful.

Medium-growing climbers

'CLIMBING ENA HARKNESS'

A vigorous climbing large-flowered (hybrid tea) rose, introduced in 1954. It will grow to 5m/16½ft high and 2.4m/8ft across. The rich scarlet, fully double, fragrant, urn-shaped flowers hang elegantly from the stems and are borne over a long period from summer to autumn. The leaves are semi-glossy. 'Climbing Ena Harkness', a sport of the bush rose 'Ena Harkness', needs a warm, sheltered site to give of its best.

'CLIMBING ICEBERG'

A climbing cluster-flowered (floribunda) rose, introduced in 1968. It will grow to 5m/16½ft or more high and across. From summer to autumn clusters of lightly scented, creamy white, cupped, double flowers are produced among abundant, glossy light green leaves. The stems are virtually thornless. 'Climbing Iceberg', a sport of the popular shrub rose 'Iceberg', is among the most reliable of modern climbers and is a good choice for clothing a wall.

■ **LEFT**
'CLIMBING PEACE'

A climbing rose, introduced in 1951, and a sport of the popular large-flowered (hybrid tea) bush rose 'Peace'. It will grow to 5m/16½ft high and 1.2m/4ft across. The large, fully double, fragrant flowers are creamy yellow flushed with pink, and appear from summer to autumn. The abundant leaves are large and glossy.

■ **RIGHT**
'DESPREZ A FLEURS JAUNES'

(syn. 'Jaune Desprez')
A climbing noisette rose, introduced in 1830, which will grow to 5m/16½ft high and across. In summer it produces fully double, quartered, fragrant, warm creamy yellow flowers that open virtually flat. The leaves are light green. Best trained against a warm wall, this rose is an exquisite climber.

■ LEFT
'GLOIRE DE DIJON'

A vigorous climbing tea rose, introduced in 1853. It will grow to 5m/16½ft high and 4m/13ft across. The striking, fully double, fragrant, quartered-rosette, buff-apricot flowers are produced over a long period from early summer to autumn. The leaves are tinged red on emergence in spring. 'Gloire de Dijon', one of the oldest climbing roses and commonly known as the old glory rose, is still widely grown; it appreciates a sunny, sheltered site.

■ BELOW
'MADAME ALFRED CARRIERE'

A climbing noisette rose, introduced in 1879, which will grow to 5m/16½ft high and 3m/10ft across. From summer to autumn the creamy white, double, cupped, fragrant flowers are freely produced on almost thornless stems. The leaves are large and pale green. 'Madame Alfred Carrière', a dependable rose, tolerates some shade and is excellent for growing into a tree or for covering a wall.

Shorter-growing climbers

■ ABOVE
'ALOHA'

A climbing large-flowered (hybrid tea) rose, introduced in 1949. It will grow to 3m/10ft high and 2.4m/8ft across. The cupped, fully double, light pink, rain-resistant flowers are borne from summer to autumn. The leaves are dark green. 'Aloha' is suitable for growing in a container.

■ ABOVE RIGHT
'BREATH OF LIFE'

(syn. 'Harquanne')
A climbing large-flowered (hybrid tea) rose, introduced in 1982. It will grow to 2.4m/8ft high and 2.1m/7ft across. From summer to autumn it bears fully double, rounded, fragrant pink flowers. This rose can be grown as a shrub with hard pruning.

■ LEFT
'CASINO'

(syn. 'Macca', 'Gerbe d'Or')
A climbing large-flowered (hybrid tea) rose, introduced in 1963. It will grow to 3m/10ft high and 2.1m/7ft across. Over a long period in summer the double, fragrant, soft-yellow flowers open from pointed, deep yellow buds. The leaves are glossy and dark green. 'Casino' appreciates a warm site sheltered from cold winds. It can be grown as a shrub with hard pruning.

■ LEFT
'CHAPLIN'S PINK CLIMBER'

A vigorous climbing rose, introduced in 1928, which will grow to 4m/13ft high and 2.4m/8ft across. From summer to autumn it produces semi-double, lightly scented, bright pink flowers with prominent golden stamens. The leaves are mid-green.

■ BELOW
'CLIMBING BLUE MOON'

A climbing large-flowered (hybrid tea) rose, introduced in 1964. It will grow to 3m/10ft high and 1.8m/6ft across. Throughout summer it produces fully double, scented, lilac-mauve flowers that appear bluer when it is grown in full sun. The leaves are glossy green. 'Climbing Blue Moon' is a sport of the large-flowered bush rose 'Blue Moon'.

■ LEFT
'CLIMBING
FRAGRANT
CLOUD'

(syn.
'Colfragrasar')
A climbing rose
which will grow
to 3m/10ft high
and 1.8m/6ft
across. From
summer to
autumn it carries
very heavily
scented, large,
coral-red flowers
amid leathery
leaves. The well-
shaped flowers
are excellent
for cutting.

■ RIGHT
'CLIMBING PASCALI'

This climbing rose, a sport of the bush
rose 'Pascali', grows to a height of
3m/10ft, with a spread of 1.5m/5ft.
From summer to autumn shapely,
creamy white buds open to fully double,
lightly scented flowers. The leaves are
large but rather sparse. 'Climbing
Pascali' provides good material for
cutting and is one the most rain-resistant
white varieties.

■ RIGHT
'CLIMBING THE QUEEN ELIZABETH'

A climbing rose, introduced in 1957, and a sport of the popular shrub rose 'Queen Elizabeth'. It will grow to about 4m/13ft high and 3m/10ft across. Shapely, high-centred, fully double, lightly scented, clear-pink flowers are freely produced from summer to autumn. The leaves are leathery and glossy.

■ LEFT
'COMPASSION'

(syn. 'Belle de Londres')
A climbing large-flowered (hybrid tea) rose, introduced in 1973, which will grow to 3m/10ft high and 2.4m/8ft across. From summer to autumn it produces shapely, rounded, fully double, sweetly scented, warm apricot-pink flowers. The leaves are dark green. 'Compassion' is excellent grown on a pillar.

■ ABOVE
'CONSTANCE SPRY'

(syn. 'Austance')
A shrub rose, introduced in 1961, suitable for training as a climber. It will grow to 3m/10ft high and across. In mid-summer it produces a profusion of large, cupped, fully double, richly scented, warm-pink flowers. The leaves are coarse and greyish-green. Despite its single flush of flowers, 'Constance Spry' is one of the most desirable of modern climbers and is spectacular at its peak; it tolerates some shade.

■ LEFT
'CRIMSON DESCANT'

A climbing rose, introduced in 1972, which will grow to 3m/10ft high and 1.2m/4ft across. From summer to autumn it produces masses of double, lightly scented, bright crimson flowers. The foliage is glossy green. 'Crimson Descant' is a reliably healthy rose, tolerates some shade, and is suitable for a pillar.

■ ABOVE
'DORTMUND'

A climbing rose which grows to 3m/10ft high and 1.8m/6ft across. It produces an abundant and reliable crop of single, bright red flowers with white eyes until autumn, if regularly deadheaded. An excellent choice for a pillar.

■ ABOVE
'DANSE DU FEU'

(syn. 'Spectacular')
A vigorous climbing rose, introduced in 1954, which will grow to 2.4m/8ft high and across. From summer to autumn it bears clusters of double, rounded, lightly scented, luminous red flowers among glossy, bronze-tinged, dark green leaves. 'Danse du Feu', a popular and free-flowering rose, is prone to blackspot.

■ RIGHT
'DUBLIN BAY'

(syn. 'Macdub')
A climbing rose, introduced in 1976, which has a height and spread of 2.1m/7ft. From summer to autumn clusters of double, lightly scented, almost fluorescent red flowers are produced amid healthy, glossy, large leaves. 'Dublin Bay' is a good choice where space is limited, since the growth tends to be upright.

■ ABOVE

'LAURA FORD'

(syn. 'Chewarvel')
A miniature climbing rose, introduced in
1990. It will grow to 2.1m/7ft high and
1.2m/4ft across. From summer to autumn
it produces clusters of small, lightly
scented, yellow flowers among small,
shiny, dark green leaves. An excellent
choice for a small garden, 'Laura Ford' is
also suitable for growing in a container.

■ RIGHT

'HANDEL'

(syn. 'Macha')
A vigorous climbing rose, introduced in
1965. It will grow to 3m/10ft high and
2.1m/7ft across. Double, urn-shaped,
lightly scented flowers with cream petals
edged with pink, are produced from mid-
summer to autumn. The dark green leaves
are tinged bronze. 'Handel' is valued for
the unique colouring of its flowers; with
hard pruning it can be grown as a shrub.
Blackspot may be a problem.

■ BELOW

'GOLDEN SHOWERS'

A climbing rose, introduced in 1957, which will grow to 3m/10ft high and 1.8m/6ft across. From summer to autumn it produces clusters of double (but with few petals), lightly scented, yellow flowers. The leaves are glossy dark green. 'Golden Showers' performs well in a variety of situations and tolerates some shade.

■ ABOVE

'HIGHFIELD'

(syn. 'Harcomp')
A climbing rose, introduced in 1981, and a sport of 'Compassion'. It will grow to 3m/10ft high and 2.4m/8ft across. From summer to autumn it produces shapely, rounded, fully double, fragrant, primrose-yellow flowers. The leaves are dark green.

■ ABOVE
'MAIGOLD'

A vigorous climbing pimpinellifolia
hybrid, introduced in 1953, which will
grow to 2.4m/8ft high and across. In early
summer semi-double, cupped, sweetly
scented, rich yellow flowers are produced
in clusters, usually in a single flush. The
leaves are leathery and glossy. 'Maigold', a
tough and hardy rose, is valued for its early
flowering and resistance to disease.

■ LEFT
'MORNING JEWEL'

A vigorous climbing rose, introduced in
1968, which will grow to 3m/10ft high
and 2.4m/8ft across. Clusters of glowing
pink, double, cupped, lightly scented
flowers are freely produced in mid-
summer; the autumn display is less
profuse. The leaves are glossy dark green.
Generally a healthy rose, 'Morning Jewel'
can be grown as a shrub with hard pruning.

■ RIGHT
× *ODORATA* 'PALLIDA'

A China rose, introduced from China
around 1752 but undoubtedly much older,
suitable for training as a climber. It will
grow to 2.4m/8ft high and 1.5m/5ft
across. From summer to early winter it
produces double, cupped, fragrant, clear
pink flowers amid elegant, pointed leaves.
Sometimes known as the old blush China
rose or Parsons' pink China rose, this
rewards careful cultivation by flowering
until the first frosts.

■ LEFT

× *ODORATA* 'MUTABILIS'

(syn. *R. chinensis*, 'Mutabilis')
A China rose of uncertain parentage, introduced from China some time before 1894, although it may be much older. It is suitable for training as a climber and will grow to 3m/10ft high and 1.8m/6ft across. The single, cupped, lightly scented flowers are borne over a long period from summer to autumn. They are of unique colouring: flame-orange in bud, they open to coppery yellow then fade to pink, the pink deepening to purple as they age. The leaves are dark green and glossy. It appreciates a warm site and in cold climates is best in full sun against a wall.

■ RIGHT

'PARKDIREKTOR RIGGERS'

A vigorous climbing rose, introduced in 1957, which will grow to 4m/13ft high and across. From summer to autumn it produces semi-double, lightly scented, glowing crimson flowers that have prominent yellow stamens. The leaves are glossy dark green. 'Parkdirektor Riggers' is valued for its disease-resistance and long flowering season.

146

■ LEFT
'PAUL'S LEMON PILLAR'

A stiffly upright climbing rose with a height and spread of 4m/13ft, sometimes more. The single flush of sumptuous, fragrant, creamy white flowers is produced in early summer. The coarse leaves are rather sparse. A rose of considerable distinction, 'Paul's Lemon Pillar' is best trained against a wall.

■ ABOVE
'PHYLLIS BIDE'

A climbing rose which grows to a height of 2.4m/8ft and 1.5m/5ft across. Throughout summer and autumn it produces clusters of dainty, salmon-pink flowers that darken with age amid glossy leaves. Of restrained habit, 'Phyllis Bide' is ideal for training against a low wall, over an arch or up a pillar.

■ ABOVE
'PINK PERPETUE'

A vigorous climbing rose, introduced in 1965, which will grow to 3m/10ft high and 2.4m/8ft across. The lightly scented flowers, which are borne from summer to autumn, are double, cupped to rosette, and have petals that are light pink with darker bases. The leaves are leathery and dark green. 'Pink Perpétué' has a spreading habit that makes it suitable for covering a wall; it can also be grown as a shrub if it is pruned hard. Rust may be a problem.

Miniature
Roses

The history of miniature roses

Until the end of the 17th century nearly all of the roses grown in European gardens flowered once only, around mid-summer. These are some of the most ancient roses: the albas, gallicas, damasks and centifolias, along with their mossy sports, the moss roses. Many are still grown and much loved to this day for their pure colours and heavenly fragrance. But the introduction of *Rosa chinensis*, the China or Bengal rose, revolutionized rose breeding in Europe, for it is this species and its variants that possessed the invaluable characteristic of repeat flowering.

As we have seen, in 1781 a pink-flowered China rose, known as the old blush China rose (now known as *R. × odorata* 'Pallida'), was introduced to the Netherlands from India. Several years later the British East India Company brought the crimson-flowered *R. semperflorens* or 'Slater's Crimson China' to Britain. The importance of these plants in rose breeding can hardly be overestimated. The genetic legacy of these two Chinese roses is expressed in almost all of the roses that flower repeatedly today.

In the early years the Chinese roses were crossed with European roses to yield the repeat-flowering Bourbons,

■ ABOVE
Rosa old blush China was one of the most important introductions, bringing repeat-flowering genes to modern roses.

■ ABOVE
'Pompon de Paris', as 'Rouletii' is now known, is the forerunner of all true miniatures. It is also sometimes known as the pygmy rose.

Portlands, noisettes, tea roses and, finally, the hybrid perpetuals, the elegant forerunners of the modern hybrid teas (now called large-flowered bush roses). The era of the modern rose began in 1867 with the introduction of the first hybrid tea, 'La France', which was probably as a result of a chance cross between a hybrid perpetual and a tea rose.

■ RIGHT
The ground cover shrub 'White Flower Carpet' produces clusters of small, double, lightly scented, white flowers from summer to autumn.

Further developments followed rapidly. By introducing the genes of *R. moschata* and *R. multiflora* to those of *R. chinensis* a new, very hardy race, the dwarf polyanthas, eventually emerged around 1900. These were first developed by the Poulsen nurseries in Denmark. The eventual result was the cluster-flowered bush rose or floribunda.

It is worth bearing in mind the origin of these roses. To be so successful in the harsh winter climates of continental and northern Europe, these compact and floriferous bushes needed to be extremely tough and hardy. This constitutional legacy is one that benefits growers of modern roses. Their descendants, the dwarf cluster-flowered bushes, also known as patio roses, are very tolerant of cold. Most derive from the crossing of cluster-flowered roses with dwarf polyanthas and miniature roses. Their group name, patio rose, is somewhat unfortunate, for although they are undoubtedly of suitable proportions for growing in pots to decorate a patio, the name scarcely begins to describe their versatility in gardens.

The origins of the true miniature rose are still mysterious, although experts agree that the original miniatures were probably diminutive sports (mutations) of a China rose. Indeed, *R. chinensis* seems to have proved a particularly valuable species. After its introduction to Europe, the earliest miniatures appear to have been grown primarily as houseplants. The discovery in 1918 by a Swiss army officer, named Roulet, of tiny roses of this type decorating the window ledges of Swiss chalets stimulated the interest of Dutch and Spanish hybridizers. The genes of 'Rouletii' (syn. *R. chinensis* var. *minima* now known as 'Pompon de Paris') are obviously present in many of the modern miniatures grown in gardens today.

The 1980s saw the advent of a new rose revolution: the creation of the so-called ground-cover roses, which reduce the need for weeding by shading out some weeds with their dense-leaved habit. Again, the term "ground-cover" does little justice to their versatility.

The development of the ground-cover roses and miniature roses has continued apace in Britain, in continental Europe and especially in the United States. Given this provenance, you can be sure that these roses will be cold-hardy in all but the most severe of climates. The increase in popularity of these small roses has gone hand-in-hand with the general reduction in the size of gardens in the latter part of the 20th century. Having found a considerable market demand, there is no doubt that their ranks will swell in future years.

■ LEFT

Trailing ground-cover roses, grown as weeping standards, can be trained both to decorate a hedge and frame an entrance.

■ ABOVE

Roses do not need to be trailing to be effective in hanging baskets, as these ground-cover roses demonstrate.

uniformity of colour and performance is an absolute requirement. This uniformity can also be put to good use when they are planted as low hedging or as edging to a border.

When grown as a single or double row flanking a path, these roses provide a low, continuous ribbon of colour that is beautiful in its own right. They also perform an invaluable design function by drawing the eye along the planting scheme, which may then terminate in an attractive focal point, such as a

rose arch, statue or tall, elegant container, where climbing roses can continue the theme.

Ground-cover roses

This group includes some of the most versatile of the smaller roses. Ground-cover roses come in two main types, both equally hardy: the compact, very bushy and slightly spreading types, such as 'Laura Ashley' (syn. 'Chewharia'); and the trailing ground-cover roses, such as 'Nozomi'

(syn. 'Heideröslein'), which have long, flexible stems, which root where they touch the ground. The spreading growth tends to form a low mound of foliage that is perfect for the front of a shrub or mixed border, mixing well with shrubs and perennials.

Ground-cover roses, especially the trailing sorts, are perfect for clothing sunny banks, especially those that are awkward and inaccessible, since most require little maintenance or pruning. Their trailing habit is displayed to great advantage if they are allowed to cascade from a height. Each flexible stem will be wreathed along its entire length with bloom for much of the summer. They can be grown over retaining walls or from the top of a terrace, planted in tall pots and urns, or in large, moss-lined hanging baskets. Many are also available as standards, grafted on to the top of a long, straight stem to give a graceful, weeping effect. Moreover, if you use them in any of these ways where they can be reflected in still water, you double their beauty instantly.

Their effectiveness as ground-cover relies on the density of their foliage to exclude light and so reduce weed growth beneath them. However, some experts consider "ground-cover" a misleading term, for some weed species continue to grow unabated during the cold months when the roses are leafless. Thorough advance preparation is therefore fundamental to success. The roses must be planted in weed-free soil and top-dressed with a weed suppressant, such as chipped bark, or planted through a membrane of landscaping fabric.

■ RIGHT
In this cottage garden, roses blend perfectly with love-in-a-mist (*Nigella damascena*).

Dwarf polyanthas, Chinas and centifolias

The small bushes in this group often have a graceful habit, with airy sprays of bloom that associate particularly well with herbaceous perennials and with other shrubs in a mixed border. They are ideal for cottage garden style plantings, and their restricted height makes them particularly suitable for low hedging, useful when you need to create barriers between different parts of the garden. They also make ideal container plants, with an elegant habit that suits a range of pots, tubs and urns. Use them to decorate a patio or courtyard, to create a focal point or to mark a change in style or level within the garden. Alternatively, pairs can be used to flank an entrance.

Most of this group of small roses, which includes the polyantha 'Cécile Brünner' (syn. 'Mignon', 'Sweetheart Rose') and its sport 'Perle d'Or' (syn. 'Yellow Cécile Brünner'), have been grown in gardens for over a century, and are hardy and reliable.

Plant Catalogue

'ANGELA RIPPON'

(syn. 'Ocarina', 'Ocaru')
A miniature bush rose with a dense-leaved, upright and bushy habit. It will grow to 45cm/18in high and 30cm/12in across. Throughout summer, it bears clusters of small, rounded, fully double flowers of deep rich salmon-pink that have a light fragrance. The healthy foliage is a glossy dark green. Good for pots, large window boxes and low edging or hedging.

The roses described on the following pages are hardy and reliable, as well as being beautiful. Most are readily available from garden centres, although a few will require a little searching out from specialist nurseries. The height and spread indicated for each plant are those that might be expected in the best growing conditions; they will, of course, depend on soil, climate and season.

■ RIGHT

'ANNA FORD'

(syn. 'Harpiccolo')
A patio rose of compact habit and with a notably good health record. It will grow to 45cm/18in high and 40cm/16in across. Clusters of vibrant orange-red, semi-double, urn-shaped flowers are produced from summer to autumn. The leaves are a glossy dark green. Good for containers, borders and low hedging.

■ RIGHT
'APRICOT SUMMER'

(syn. 'Korpapiro')

A patio rose of neat, compact habit, which grows to 40cm/16in high and across. Throughout the summer months there is a profusion of small, double, rounded, salmon-apricot blooms in many-flowered clusters. Useful for pots, window boxes, beds and border edging.

■ BELOW
'BABY LOVE'

(syn. 'Scrivluv')

A bushy, upright patio rose, which will grow to 1m/3ft high and 75cm/2½ft across. Clusters of cupped, single, short-stemmed, bright yellow flowers appear throughout summer. The dense foliage is mid-green. An exceptionally healthy and floriferous rose, perfect for beds, borders and low hedging.

■ ABOVE
'AVON'

(syn. 'Poulmulti')

A low, creeping ground-cover rose of compact habit, which grows to 30cm/12in high and 1m/3ft across. The creeping stems are wreathed with clusters of flat, semi-double, lightly scented blush-pink then pearly white flowers from summer to autumn. Ideal for clothing awkward banks or for a flowering cascade over a wall.

■ BELOW
'CAPTAIN SCARLET'

A stiffly upright miniature climbing rose, which will grow to 2.1m/7ft high and 1.2cm/4ft across. It has a compact habit with good disease-resistance; unlike most other, larger climbers it remains clothed to the base with flowers and foliage. The semi-double, rounded, bright red, rather muddled flowers are produced repeatedly from summer to autumn, set off beautifully by dark green foliage that becomes flushed with copper tints in cold weather.

■ ABOVE
'BALLERINA'

A compact polyantha shrub rose, one of the older small roses, bred in 1937. It will grow to 1.5m/5ft high and 1m/3ft across. It has a compact, leafy, upright habit and bears wide clusters of cupped, single, pale pink, white-eyed blooms throughout summer into autumn. A notably floriferous award-winner, but with little scent, it is ideal for borders and low hedging and makes a good specimen for small gardens.

■ RIGHT
'BROADLANDS'

(syn. 'Tanmirson')
A vigorous, spreading ground-cover rose, which will grow to 1m/3ft high and the same or more across. The low mounds of glossy, dark green foliage are wreathed in double, rounded, soft sulphur-yellow, sweetly scented flowers throughout summer into autumn. The colour yellow is unusual among ground-cover roses. It is ideal for clothing awkward banks or for the front of a border.

■ ABOVE
'CITY LIGHTS'

(syn. 'Poulgan')
A vigorous patio rose, growing to
60cm/2ft high and across. Wide
clusters of perfectly formed, urn-
shaped, fully double, rich yellow
blooms are shaded with apricot at
their centres. The foliage is dark
green. Flowering throughout
summer, it is perfect for urns,
troughs and pots. Its neat habit also
suits border edging and low hedging.

■ RIGHT
'CIDER CUP'

(syn. 'Dicladida')
A patio rose of compact, bushy habit,
which grows to 45cm/18in high and
30cm/12in across. Many-flowered
clusters of small, double, high-
pointed blooms of a lovely warm
apricot-pink are produced
throughout summer and autumn.
The dense foliage is glossy. The neat,
upright habit is well suited to pots,
as a standard and for low hedging.

■ RIGHT

'CONSERVATION'

(syn. 'Cocdimple')
A notably healthy patio rose of dense, bushy
habit, which will grow to 45cm/18in high and
across. A profusion of cupped, semi-double
flowers of warm apricot-pink borne in well-
filled clusters from summer to autumn. The
small leaves are glossy. A neat but vigorous
grower, it is perfectly suited to containers (the
colour complements natural stone and
terracotta particularly well) and as low edging.

■ LEFT

'CLIMBING ORANGE
SUNBLAZE'

**(syn. 'Climbing Orange
Meillandina', 'Meijikatarsar')**
An aptly named miniature climber, a
climbing sport of 'Orange Sunblaze',
which will grow to 1.5m/5ft high and
70cm/28in across. Fully double, brilliant,
blazing orange-red, rounded flowers are
produced from summer to autumn and set
off to perfection against bright green
foliage. It has a well-branched, upright
habit and is perfect for wall training where
space is limited.

■ RIGHT
'CRIMSON GEM'

A vigorous miniature bush rose, which will grow to 45cm/18in high and across. It is clothed throughout summer in perfectly formed, rounded, double, deep rich red flowers set off against dark, glossy foliage. 'Crimson Gem' is a perfect container rose, especially good in large window boxes and containers, and is equally at home edging a bed or border.

■ ABOVE
'FESTIVAL'

(syn. 'Kordialo')
A patio rose, which will grow to 60cm/2ft high and 50cm/20in across, and which has a neat, rounded habit. The sumptuously coloured crimson-scarlet double, rounded blooms open to reveal a centre of gold and silver, and the pale silvery petal reverse adds greatly to its charm. The luxuriant foliage is glossy dark green. Perfect for pots, especially in pairs set to flank a doorway.

■ LEFT
'DARLING FLAME'

(syn. 'Meilucca', 'Minuetto')
A colourful miniature bush, growing to 40cm/16in high and 30cm/12in across. It produces clusters of small, rounded, double blooms of vibrant orange-red with golden anthers. It has upright growth and glossy foliage and, although free-flowering, is slightly susceptible to blackspot. Creates a brilliant ribbon of colour when used as edging, and is ideal for containers.

■ ABOVE
'FRESH PINK'

This petite polyantha rose, which grows to
0.6–1m/2–3ft high and across, produces
large trusses of rounded, double, clear pink
flowers very freely from summer to
autumn. The graceful habit is displayed to
good effect in large urns or other
containers, and it is equally at home
lending grace and pure colour to a mixed
or shrub border.

■ RIGHT
'GLORIA MUNDI'

A compact polyantha rose, growing to
70cm/28in high and across, with large
clusters of cupped, brilliant orange-red,
semi-double flowers produced almost
continuously throughout the summer
months. It can be used as low hedging or
bedding and in containers and, unlike
many roses, it will tolerate a little shade
and poor soils, although flowering will be
less profuse in these conditions.

■ LEFT

'HAKUUN'

A low-growing patio rose of neat, rounded habit, which grows to 40cm/16in high and 45cm/18in across. It bears exceptionally lovely, creamy white, double, rounded flowers, buff-tinted in bud and at the petal base, in well-filled clusters from summer to autumn. It has a pleasing light fragrance. This healthy rose would be perfect in containers sited where the flowers can be appreciated at close quarters. It is also good for cut flowers.

■ RIGHT

'HAMPSHIRE'

(syn. 'Korhamp')

A dense and compact bush, which will grow to 30cm/12in high and 60cm/2ft across. From summer to autumn it is clothed with clusters of stunning, single, slightly cupped, scarlet blooms with a white eye and a central boss of golden stamens. The flowers are followed by scarlet hips in autumn. Equally at home in containers or in open ground in beds and borders.

■ LEFT

'INDIAN SUNBLAZE'

(syn. 'Carol-Jean')

A patio rose, growing to 45cm/18in high and across. The rounded, fully double, deep pink flowers are produced repeatedly from summer to autumn above fresh green foliage. 'Indian Sunblaze' is excellent for containers of all sorts and as low edging to paths and borders.

■ RIGHT
'HAREWOOD'

(syn. 'Taninaso)
A patio or ground-cover rose
which will grow to 60cm/2ft
high and 1m/3ft across. The
semi-double, soft pink
flowers, which open flat to
reveal yellow stamens, are
produced in clusters from
summer to autumn.
'Harewood' is suitable for
banks or containers.

■ BELOW
'KENT'

**(syn. 'White Cover',
'Poulcov, Pyrenees')**
A compact and spreading
ground-cover shrub rose,
which grows to 45cm/18in
high and 1m/3ft across.
Smothered in large trusses of
cupped, short-stemmed, semi-
double, pure white flowers
from summer to autumn, it is
perfect for sunny banks or for
the front of mixed and shrub
borders. It is also stunning if
grown to cascade from tall
containers or retaining walls. It
has an excellent health record
and good weather-resistance.

■ ABOVE
'LADY PENELOPE'

A stiffly upright miniature climber of neat habit,
which grows to 2.1m/7ft high and 1.2m/4ft across.
Rounded, fully double, salmon-pink flowers are
borne repeatedly from summer to autumn. A healthy
rose that remains clothed to the base with flowers
and foliage, it is ideal for walls in confined spaces
and for smaller gardens.

■ ABOVE
'MAGIC CARPET'

(syn. 'Jaclover')
A ground-cover rose which grows to 40cm/16in high and 1m/3ft across.
Clusters of semi-double, sparkling lilac-pink flowers are carried in profusion
from summer to autumn. The foliage is very disease-resistant. 'Magic Carpet'
is valued for its use as ground-cover but it can also be grown successfully in
troughs and containers.

■ LEFT
'MINI METRO'

(syn. 'Finstar', 'Rufin')
A miniature bush rose, which will grow to 40cm/16in high and 25cm/10in
across. Clusters of well-formed, rounded, fully double, apricot-orange flowers
open to reveal golden stamens. The foliage is fresh green. Flowering throughout
summer, it is ideal for pots and window boxes and other containers.

■ ABOVE

'MR BLUEBIRD'

A miniature China rose of bushy, compact habit, which grows to 30cm/12in high and 25cm/10in across. Airy sprays of many small, cupped, semi-double, white-eyed flowers in shades of reddish-purple are borne from summer to autumn. With such a novel and unusual colour, this healthy little rose is perfect for window boxes, pots and other containers, or as an edging to beds and borders.

■ RIGHT

'NICE DAY'

(syn. 'Chewsea', 'Patio Queen') A miniature climbing rose, which grows to 2.1m/7ft high and 1m/3ft across. Clusters of small, double, urn-shaped flowers of warm peachy pink with a light sweet scent are borne from summer to autumn. 'Nice Day' is excellent for a low wall or trellis where space is confined. The perfectly formed buds are ideal as buttonholes and for flower arrangements.

■ LEFT

'NORTHAMPTONSHIRE'

(syn. 'Mattdor')

A vigorous, low-growing ground-cover rose, which will grow to 45cm/18in high and 1m/3ft across. Dainty sprays of perfectly formed, cupped, soft pink flowers are borne from summer to autumn. It has dense, glossy dark green foliage. This spreading rose has an excellent health record and is good for clothing sunny banks, for trailing over retaining walls, or for the front of a mixed border.

■ RIGHT

'ORANGES AND LEMONS'

(syn. 'Macoranlem')

A compact cluster-flowered rose, which will grow to 80cm/32in high and 60cm/2ft across. It bears heavy clusters of rounded, double flowers from summer to autumn, striped and partly coloured scarlet-orange on a creamy golden-yellow ground. The shiny dark green leaves are flushed copper when young. Perhaps too large for all but the most substantial of containers, this sunny little rose is ideal for low hedging, and massed plantings in beds and borders.

■ LEFT

'ORANGE SUNBLAZE'

(syn. 'Meijikatar', 'Orange Meillandina')

A bushy miniature rose, growing to 30cm/12in high and across. Profuse clusters of small, cupped, semi-double flowers of brilliant, vivid orange-red with golden centres are produced from summer to autumn. The ample foliage is bright green. Excellent for containers of all sorts, and as low edging to paths and borders.

■ BELOW
'OXFORDSHIRE'

(syn. 'Korfullwind')
An award-winning, spreading ground-cover rose, which grows
to 60cm/2ft high and 1.5m/5ft across. Cascading stems are
wreathed in double clear pink rounded flowers almost
continuously from summer to autumn. Ideal for sunny banks,
'Oxfordshire' also looks stunning when grown as a standard
or in hanging baskets.

■ RIGHT
'PERLE D'OR'

(syn. 'Yellow Cécile
Brünner')
One of the older small roses,
this polyantha bush has a
dense habit of growth, and
will grow to 1.2m/4ft high
and 1m/3ft across. Dainty
sprays of scented, diminutive
but exquisitely formed, urn-
shaped flowers of creamy
honey-yellow flushed with
pink last from summer to
autumn. There is ample, dark
green foliage. Almost
thornless, it is ideal for a
mixed border or for large
urns and containers.

■ ABOVE
'PEEK A BOO'

(syn. 'Brass Ring',
'Dicgrow')
A neat, cushion-forming
patio rose, with a slightly
spreading habit, which will
grow to 45cm/18in high
and across. Well-filled
clusters of small but
beautifully formed,
rounded, double flowers of
a gentle, rich peachy
apricot gradually fade to
pink as they mature. 'Peek
a Boo' is perfect for
containers and urns and for
cutting to use in flower
arrangements.

'PRETTY POLLY'

**(syn. 'Meitonje', 'Sweet Sunblaze',
'Pink Symphony')**
A dense, rounded and well-named
miniature rose, which will grow to
40cm/16in high and 45cm/18in across.
Blooming from summer to autumn, the
beautifully formed, rounded, fully double
flowers, borne in well-filled clusters, have a
light sweet scent and are of a particularly
pretty clear pink. The plentiful foliage is
dark, glossy green. It is particularly good in
terracotta containers and window boxes or
grown as low edging.

'QUEEN MOTHER'

(syn. 'Korquemu')
A delightful patio rose, which grows
to 40cm/16in high and 60cm/2ft
across. Clusters of cupped, semi-
double flowers with slightly wavy
petals of a delicate, soft clear pink
are borne in profusion throughout
summer into autumn. The plentiful
foliage is dark, glossy green. Ideal
for containers, including hanging
baskets and large window boxes.

'RED ACE'

(syn. 'Amanda', 'Amruda')
One of the most sumptuous reds among the miniature roses, this little bush grows to 30cm/12in high and 30cm/12in across. It has a neat, leafy habit and produces clusters of rounded, semi-double, rich crimson blooms from summer to autumn. 'Red Ace' makes a fine edging to a border, a dramatic massed planting and a beautiful specimen for containers. The flowers are also perfect for cutting.

'RED MEIDILAND'

(syn. 'Meineble', 'Rouge Meillandécar')
A dense, compact ground-cover rose with a height of 75cm/2½ft and a spread of 1.5m/5ft. Clusters of relatively large, deep red, single, cupped flowers with white centres and a boss of golden stamens are borne almost continuously from summer to autumn. The flowers are followed by small red hips. 'Red Meidiland' is suitable for the front of a shrub or mixed border, and is particularly useful for clothing sunny banks or trailing over a retaining wall.

■ LEFT

'RISE 'N' SHINE'

(syn. 'Golden Meillandina', 'Golden Sunblaze')
A miniature bush rose of neat, compact habit, which will grow to 40cm/16in high and 25cm/ 10in across. Clusters of small but well-formed, fully double, urn-shaped, sunny yellow flowers with pointed petals are produced from summer right through to autumn. Use in containers of all sorts and as low edging in formal beds and borders.

■ RIGHT

'SCARLET MEIDILAND'

(syn. 'Meikrotal')
A ground-cover shrub rose, growing to 1m/3ft high and 1.8m/6ft across. Large, heavy clusters of many small, cherry-red, rounded, double blooms with golden stamens are produced in abundance from summer onwards; the autumn flushes of flower are notably profuse. It is suitable for the middle ranks of a shrub or mixed border, and for low hedging and containers; it even tolerates light shade.

■ LEFT

'SUN HIT'

(syn. 'Poulsun')
A compact patio rose of upright habit, growing to 45cm/18in high and across. Sunny golden-yellow, fully double, urn-shaped blooms, with moderately good scent, are borne in great profusion from summer to autumn. Bred as a pot-rose, its small stature is ideally suited to containers and window boxes and it can also be brought into the house when in bloom. Also available as a standard.

'SUSSEX'

(syn. 'Poulav')

A vigorous ground-cover rose, growing to 45cm/18in high and 1m/3ft across. Masses of flowers are borne from early summer to autumn. The fully double, rounded, neatly formed flowers are a soft apricot-pink. 'Sussex' is ideal grown on a sunny bank.

■ ABOVE

'SURREY'

(syn. 'Korlanum', 'Sommerwind', 'Vent d'été')

A robust ground-cover rose, which looks superb in large containers, in borders or as a specimen. It will grow to 1m/3ft high and 1.2m/4ft across. It has a leafy habit, producing dense mounds of foliage and long stems wreathed with abundant clusters of double, cupped, warm pink flowers from summer to autumn.

■ RIGHT

'SWANY'

(syn. 'Meiburenac')

A bushy, spreading and very elegant ground-cover rose, which grows to 1m/3ft high and 1.5m/5ft across. The plentiful glossy dark green, slightly bronzed foliage is a perfect foil to the wreathing clusters of flat, double, pure white flowers. It is charming in containers – especially in a formal setting – and in mixed borders.

■ ABOVE
'SWEET MAGIC'

(syn. 'Dicmagic')

An attractive award-winning patio rose, which grows to 40cm/16in high and across. Full clusters of scented, double, rounded soft apricot-orange and yellow flowers are borne freely from summer to autumn. The dense foliage is bright green. A perfect container specimen and ideal for edging.

■ RIGHT
'SWEET DREAM'

(syn. 'Fryminicot')

A neat, upright patio rose, growing to 40cm/16in high and 35cm/14in across. It has a moderate scent and a very attractive 'old-fashioned' flower form. The fully double, warm apricot-pink flowers are in quartered-rosette form and borne in abundant clusters from summer to autumn. 'Sweet Dream' is particularly elegant in containers or as ribbon edging to paths and beds.

■ RIGHT
'THE FAIRY'

A dwarf polyantha rose growing to 60cm/2ft or more high and across. It is a deserving award-winner which blooms almost continuously from late summer to autumn. It has a dense, spreading, cushion-like habit, and bears dainty sprays of small, fully double, rosette-shaped flowers in pale pink. Lovely in a shrub or mixed border and elegant in containers, with a good health record.

■ LEFT
'TOP MARKS'

(syn. 'Fryministar')
A neat, cushion-forming patio rose, growing to 40cm/16in high and 45cm/18in across. It bears well-filled clusters of double, rounded, brilliant orange-vermilion flowers from summer to autumn. The glossy foliage is abundant. An award-winning rose, it is suitable for edging borders and bedding and makes a striking specimen in containers.

■ RIGHT
'WARM WELCOME'

(syn. 'Chewizz')
A glossy-leaved miniature climber, growing to 2.1m/7ft high and across. Small, semi-double, urn-shaped, bright orange-vermilion flowers are borne freely and almost continuously from summer to autumn. Good for walls in small courtyards or where space is restricted.

■ ABOVE
'WHITE CECILE BRUNNER'

A diminutive polyantha bush with a height and spread of 1m/3ft. Dainty sprays of sweetly scented, beautifully fully double, urn-shaped, white flowers, faintly peach-tinted, are borne almost continuously from summer to autumn. There is plentiful dark green foliage. Almost thornless, it is ideal for a mixed border or for large urns and other substantial containers. A perfect buttonhole flower.

■ ABOVE
'WHITE FLOWER CARPET'

(syn. 'Noaschnee')
A dense, ground-cover shrub, which will grow to 75cm/2½ft high and 1.2m/4ft across. Mounds of dark, semi-evergreen foliage offset clusters of large, cupped, semi-double white flowers, which are borne from summer to autumn. Excellent on a sunny bank, as a standard or trailing over a wall. It has a good health record. There are red and pink forms too.

■ LEFT
'WILTSHIRE'

(syn. 'Kormuse')
A spreading ground-cover shrub, which will grow to 60cm/2ft high and 1.2m/4ft across. The dense glossy foliage is almost obscured by large clusters of lightly scented, rounded, double, reddish-pink flowers, which are borne from summer to autumn. A good rose for banks or planters.

Buying roses

Choosing new roses for the garden is one of the most enjoyable of all gardening activities, for it carries with it the anticipation of many years of pleasure from these generally long-lived shrubs. It is most important to consider the space that you have available and to select a rose variety of a suitable size so that it will not rapidly outgrow the allotted space. Proportion becomes all the more important if you wish to grow roses in containers.

There are several ways to make your selection, all of them pleasurable. You can look through gardening books and specialist rose catalogues at leisure by the fireside while you plan your plantings for the following season, or you can visit garden centres to make your selection. But perhaps the best way of selecting roses is to visit gardens in your locality, where they can be observed in growth and flower, so that you can take note of any that attract your attention. Many specialist nurseries have rose gardens attached to the nursery and encourage buyers to visit them during the summer.

■ RIGHT.
Many specialist nurseries have extensive rose gardens to display their wares and to help you make your choice.

Ideally, you should make several visits – this is, after all, no great hardship – so that you can check on their continuity of flowering performance and their overall health and vigour. In any rose collection you will notice individual cultivars that are markedly more free-flowering or healthy and disease-resistant. If any of these roses suit your purpose, you would be well advised to grow them in preference to those that perform less well – good disease-resistance does much to reduce the necessity of

repeated applications of chemical pesticides and fungicides.

Once you have decided on a rose that appeals to you and that suits the location and the purpose for which it is to be used, you have to set about finding it. Many garden centres carry a wide range of container-grown roses, and, with luck, the one you want will be in stock. Buying in this way has the advantage of allowing you to check the plants over yourself before purchase and select the most healthy specimen.

If you cannot find the rose you want at a garden centre, you need to look to a specialist supplier, preferably one that is a member of your national Rose Growers' Association. Most national rose societies produce 'who grows what' booklets, which list roses and the nurseries that supply them. Many national horticultural societies also sponsor publications of general plant lists and supplying nurseries. These leaflets are absolutely indispensable when you are trying to track down the lesser known cultivars.

You can buy happily from a reputable nursery, either directly or by mail order, for they strive constantly to produce good, healthy stock and will guarantee that their plants are well grown and true to name. Most nurseries will replace without quibble any plants that you find are unsatisfactory when your order arrives.

Roses are sold either as container-grown or bare-root plants – that is, those that have been lifted from the open ground while dormant and the roots shaken free of soil. Both types eventually make equally good plants, although container-grown roses usually establish more quickly.

Whichever type of rose you buy, good soil preparation before planting is essential if the rose is to perform well, and will considerably minimize maintenance of the plant later on.

■ ABOVE
R. 'Cécile Brünner' is a perennial favourite; healthy and floriferous, it is perfect in this elegant container.

Bare-root plants

Most growers who sell by mail order supply their roses as bare-root plants. They are usually available only between autumn and early spring. Although there may be a delay between ordering your plants and delivery, a huge range is available to you, including rare varieties.

The roses are usually dispatched in specially designed padded envelopes. The roots are wrapped in a polythene bag containing peat or a similar material to keep them moist. You can store the roses unopened for up to six weeks in a dark, cool, frost-free place.

Bare-root roses must be ordered in advance and planted in the autumn or spring.

■ ABOVE
Mail-order companies usually have a large selection of bare-rooted rose varieties.

Container-grown plants

Roses sold in containers are lifted from the field, potted up and grown on. They are available at garden centres throughout the growing season. Garden centres usually prefer to sell plants that are in full growth in containers, but they offer a much smaller choice and only the most popular varieties are likely to be available. Many gardeners find container-grown roses more convenient than bare-root plants, although they are more expensive.

When you are buying a container-grown rose, choose one that is growing evenly, with sturdy, well-spaced stems, and that has a well-balanced appearance. It should be well clothed in ample, healthy foliage that is of good colour. Avoid any plant with sparse or yellowed foliage or one that has evidence of leaf drop, which may indicate that the plant has been starved of nutrients or moisture. Such a rose will not establish well.

If possible, check that it is not pot-bound by sliding the plant from its container so that you can see the root system. The container should be well filled with healthy roots, and the growing medium should be evenly moist – neither dry nor waterlogged.

■ ABOVE
Roses sold in containers are usually in full growth.

If the roots are congested and tightly coiled around the pot, reject it. The roots will probably continue to grow in a spiral, and such plants will establish only slowly, if at all.

Look for signs of disease or pest attack, especially aphids, which generally cluster at the soft shoot tips, and blackspot and rust, which infect the foliage, and reject any plant that is dying back. The presence of a few weed seedlings on the surface of the compost is of no consequence, but a mat of liverworts or mosses suggests that the plant has been in its pot for too long and has exhausted the

nutrients in the compost, or that the plant has been waterlogged.

Although the preferred planting season is between late autumn and early spring, garden centres may have roses in stock throughout much of the growing season, and container-grown roses can be planted at any time of year except when the ground is frozen or waterlogged or during periods of drought in summer.

If you buy during the summer months, the roses will almost certainly be in flower and should be rigorously deadheaded, and pruned where necessary, before planting.

In addition, remember that if you plant in late spring or during the summer months you will need to water the plants thoroughly until they are established, paying particular attention to this during dry weather.

■ ABOVE
If possible, slide a container-grown rose from its container before buying so that you can check that the root system is healthy. The roots should fill the pot but should not be so crowded that they spiral around on themselves.

Planting in open ground

Most roses grow best in full sun but with some protection from wind. Very exposed sites are suitable only for the tough rugosas, which will also tolerate some degree of shade, although flowering is less profuse. A few roses tolerate dappled shade, although growth and flowering will be less vigorous. No rose will perform well in deep shade.

Good air circulation around the plants is important and lessens the likelihood of mildew and other fungal diseases. Consider the spread of the full-grown rose before you plant. Even roses intended to make a hedge

should be placed at least 1m/3ft apart. Planting too close to other shrubs will also limit the moisture and nutrients available to both plants.

Before planting, the site should be prepared thoroughly by digging and forking it over to break up and aerate the soil. Remove any large stones you come across. Organic matter greatly improves the texture of all soil, opening up heavy soil that clogs by binding it into crumbs, while aiding water retention on light, sandy ground. Fork in garden compost or farmyard manure at the rate of about one bucketful per square metre/yard.

Take great care to completely remove all trace of weeds, especially perennial weeds such as couch grass and ground elder. Weeds are much easier to eradicate before the rose is planted, as the roots of the two plants quickly become entangled.

Bare-root roses should be planted as soon after receipt as possible, preferably during a mild spell. If the ground is unworkable, because it is frozen or waterlogged, the rose can be stored unopened for up to six weeks in a cool, dark, frost-free place. When you are ready to plant, remove the packaging and cut back any damaged

PLANTING A BARE-ROOT ROSE

1 Dig a hole large enough to take the roots when they are spread out and deep enough not to bend them. Incorporate garden compost or well-rotted manure in the base if not already added to the soil when the bed was prepared.

2 Work a handful of bonemeal into the planting hole (wear gloves), then spread out the roots evenly, with the plant placed centrally. If the roots grow in just one direction, do not bend them, but plant the rose to one side of the hole.

3 Trickle the soil between the roots, shaking the plant occasionally as the hole is filled to settle the soil. Tread around the base of the plant to firm the soil, and make sure the budding is completely covered to prevent suckers.

or twiggy growth. Lightly trim the root, then soak the rose for about an hour in a bucket of water.

Container-grown roses can be planted at any time of year, except when the ground is frozen, waterlogged or during periods of drought. If you cannot plant immediately, keep the rose in a sheltered place and water regularly.

It is a complete myth that roses cannot be grown in soil where roses have previously been grown. It is now believed that roses enjoy a relationship with beneficial underground fungi that attach themselves to the roots and facilitate the up-take of water – and hence nutrients – from the soil. The fungi belong to a group known as mycorrhizal fungi, and they are now available commercially in sachets for adding to planting holes. They are particularly useful for helping roses establish on poor quality or virgin soils, and on soils from which older roses have been removed.

Once planted, a rose should be watered regularly until it is established. Adding a top-dressing such as chipped bark will help keep water evaporation to a minimum, and also help in the suppression of weeds.

Roses planted in the spring should quickly put forward new shoots, and may flower the following year.

PLANTING A CONTAINER-GROWN ROSE

1 Excavate a hole approximately twice the width of the container and a little deeper. Break up the soil in the bottom with a fork, incorporating humus-forming material, such as garden compost or well-rotted manure, if this has not already been done in the general preparation of the bed.

2 Remove the rose from its pot. Gently tease out some of the roots from around the edge to encourage them to grow out into the surrounding soil, then position the rootball in the hole. Lay a cane across the hole to check the depth, adding or removing soil as necessary.

3 The graft union (that point where the rose was budded on to its rootstock) should be about 2.5cm/1in below the level of the surrounding bed. Backfill with soil and firm in with your foot to ensure there are no large air pockets where the roots will dry out.

4 If you are planting in spring or early summer, apply a general garden fertilizer or one formulated for roses, and fork it in lightly. Water well, then mulch with more organic material, such as garden compost or chipped bark, to reduce water evaporation and suppress weeds.

Using a trellis

A trellis can be made of wood, plastic or some other synthetic material. The sturdiest types are best, since most climbing roses are vigorous plants that can pull down a flimsy structure. If you opt for a wood trellis make sure that it has been pressure-treated with preservative so that it will not rot. There are now a wide choice of colours available to stain wood if the trellis is not to your liking, but make sure that any stain you use is not toxic to plants. Heavy duty trellis is available at builder's merchants as well as garden centres.

Large trellis panels can be used in conjunction with fence panels or on their own to make a free standing screen. In both cases they should be nailed to timber uprights that are embedded in the ground, either in concrete or in special metal supports.

Any trellis placed against a wall should be mounted on battens to ensure adequate air circulation between the plant and the wall. This will minimize the risk of air-borne fungal diseases such as mildew. Battens also make it possible to remove the rose from the wall if you need to paint or repair the wall at a later date. Remember that the battens should also be treated with a plant-friendly wood preservative.

USING A TRELLIS

1 Decide on the best position for the trellis on the wall and drill holes at suitable intervals to take the battens. Tap in plugs to take the screws.

2 Screw the battens to the wall using rust-proof screws.

4 Fork over the planting area, thoroughly working in organic matter such as spent mushroom compost.

3 Check the position of the trellis and fix it firmly to the battens.

5 Dig a hole at least 45cm/18in from the wall. Fork in a handful of bonemeal at the bottom of the hole.

6 Check the planting depth. You should aim to cover the graft union. Plant the rose so that it is just below the level of the soil.

7 Remove the rose from its pot and tease out some of the roots. This will help them grow quickly into the surrounding soil and let the rose become established.

8 Position the rose in the hole, angling the top growth towards the wall and fanning out the roots away from the wall. Backfill with soil.

9 Firm the rose in with your feet to eliminate any pockets of air around the roots. Gently pull on the stem to check that the rose is securely planted.

10 Cut back any dead or damaged growth to healthy wood, but leave longer, healthy stems unpruned. Remove any faded flowers.

11 If the stems are long enough, fan them out horizontally and tie them loosely to the trellis. Water well. If you are planting in spring, fork in some fertilizer.

12 Correctly planted, the rose should quickly establish and will soon produce vigorous new shoots that can be trained to the trellis.

Pl
more
ordin
O
to co
final
amou
availa
is ess
top h
or da
plant
roots
rose
W
grow
estab
main

3 P
ce
drive i
centre
stake
below

Planting a climbing rose in a container

Although most climbing roses are unsuitable for growing in containers, there are several modern hybrids that make excellent plants for containers. All miniature climbing roses can be used for this purpose, and are the ideal plants to liven up a patio, terrace or roof garden. Miniature roses bear clusters of small, usually double flowers similar to those of true miniature and patio roses. They make plants no more than 2.1m/7ft high when grown in the open border, and when grown in a container, they are unlikely to exceed 1.5m/5ft in height.

A climbing rose in a container can be pruned and trained in the same way as a climbing rose in the garden, but for optimum performance, pay more attention to watering and feeding. Water freely during the growing season. At the height of summer you will need to water at least once, possibly even twice, a day. Feed with a specially formulated rose fertilizer at the start of the season to encourage flower production, and then again after the first flush of flowers. For added vigour, spray the plant regularly with a foliar feed.

Roses should not be fed after mid-summer, since this promotes sappy growth that will not ripen fully before winter and will therefore be susceptible to frost damage and may be liable to disease.

PLANTING A ROSE IN A CONTAINER

1 Cover drainage holes at the base of the container with stones or gravel to improve the drainage. It will also improve stability. Begin to fill the container with compost (soil mix).

2 Check the planting depth by standing the rose in its container on the compost. Make sure that the graft union is covered with compost and leave a gap of about 2.5cm/1in below the rim of the container to allow for watering.

3 Ease the rose out of its container and tease out the roots with a hand fork so that they grow away quickly.

4 Set the rose in position in the centre of the container and begin to backfill with the growing medium of your choice.

5 Once the correct level has been reached, firm the compost with your hands and water the rose well.

6 Insert canes or bamboo around the edge of the container, pushing them down to the base for maximum stability. An odd number of canes looks best.

7 Tie the tops of the canes together securely to create a wigwam over the container. Alternatively, use a proprietary wigwam support.

8 Run wires or string around the canes at intervals of about 20cm/8in, either as separate rounds or in a continuous spiral. As the rose grows, tie the stems in with wire ties or horticultural string.

9 To provide winter interest when the rose is not in bloom, plant winter pansies or underplant with ivies and a selection of dwarf spring bulbs for welcome spring colour.

Climbing roses in a container can be grown in two ways. They can be trained against a wall to make a spectacular display, or grown up canes set in the container for a free-standing feature.

To train a climber against a wall, first attach a trellis to the wall. The container the plant is in should be considered. Halved half-barrels made of wood are particularly suitable for the purpose because they have flat backs and can be stood directly against the wall. Alternatively, a rose trained on a wigwam of canes can be moved around at will. It can feature prominently when in bloom, and moved elsewhere in the winter.

Whichever method you choose, select a container that is large enough to allow a good root run. Stability is an important factor, so the container should be heavy enough to support the top growth, which is likely to be substantial once the rose is mature. Light plastic containers are not generally suitable. A heavy, loam-based, high-fertility compost (soil mix) is best. Peat or coir-based composts are suitable, although they are difficult to re-wet if they dry out.

SUITABLE CLIMBING AND RAMBLING ROSES FOR CONTAINERS
'Casino'
'Céline Forestier'
'Climbing Orange Sunblaze'
'Dublin Bay'
'Golden Showers'
'Good as Gold'
'Laura Ford'
'Maigold'
'Nice Day'
'Phyllis Bide'
'Swan Lake'
'Warm Welcome'
'White Cockade'

Pruning

Pruning a rose refreshes the plant and maintains an open, vase-shaped habit. It also promotes free air circulation through the plant, minimizing the risk of mildew and other fungal diseases. There are no hard and fast rules for pruning: be guided by your own judgement and by the way the rose is growing. Very vigorous roses often achieve their true potential only when left mostly to their own devices. Conversely, some weak-growing roses benefit from regular hard pruning.

Bear in mind a few basic principles. Pruning always stimulates vigorous new growth, which arises from the growth bud nearest to the cut. To promote even, balanced growth, prune straggly, weak stems hard but trim vigorous stems only lightly. If in doubt, prune lightly. You can always prune again later. Roses are, on the whole, forgiving plants. Provided you water, feed and mulch well after pruning you are unlikely to do any lasting harm to the plant, no matter what pruning policy you follow.

■ RIGHT (CLOCKWISE FROM TOP LEFT)
Bypass secateurs (pruning shears), anvil secateurs (pruning shears) and long-handled pruners (loppers or lopping shears) are all useful garden tools.

Secateurs (pruners) are suitable for most rose pruning, but you may need loppers (long-handled pruners) or a pruning saw to cut through the thick stems of older plants. Always wear gloves to protect your hands.

Use well-maintained tools with clean, sharp blades. Blunt blades will tear and snag the wood, providing an entry point for disease. After use, clean the blades with an oily rag.

Timing

When you prune your roses is a matter of judgement, depending to some extent on the local climate. In principle, you can prune at any time when the rose is dormant, from late autumn to late winter. In many areas, however, the climate is unpredictable

and an early prune – after a warm, wet spell towards the end of winter, for example – can result in a rush of sappy growth that will be damaged by an unexpected late, hard frost. The damage is seldom lasting, but growth will be checked, and you will have to prune again to remove the frosted stems. Where winters are harsh, therefore, delay pruning until early spring. You can also prune late to delay flowering. If the rose is in a container, you can prune as soon as the days begin to lengthen, bringing the plant under glass for early flowers (known as forcing). Commercial growers who exhibit at spring horticultural shows regularly force their plants in this way. Extra heat and light may also be necessary.

Renovation

Very old, neglected roses that have accumulated a quantity of unproductive wood can be given a new lease of life by hard pruning.

In late winter or early spring, cut the oldest, thickest stems back to ground level. Shorten the remainder to within 15–30cm/6–12in of the ground. Feed the plant well, water and mulch. New growth will be vigorous, but it is likely to be a year

or two before the flowering capacity
is fully restored. However, if the rose
does not make good growth during
the season following renovation, it is
beyond salvation.

Making the cuts

Growth buds lie alternately on rose
stems. Because the new growth will
arise from the bud nearest the cut,
prune to a bud that faces in the
direction you want the new shoot to
grow. Cut just above the bud, angling
away from the emerging growth.
Remove all diseased, damaged or
dead wood, and also any stems that
cross or are badly placed. On newly
planted roses, cut back the remaining
stems lightly to stimulate fresh
growth. On established plants, cut
back to ground level any old, woody,
unproductive stems. If the rose is
weak-growing, cut back the
remaining stems by up to two-thirds.
On vigorous roses, trim back lightly.
A selective approach is often best,
whereby you remove some stems,
shorten others by a third or more,
and leave the remainder unpruned or
lightly trimmed.

■ RIGHT
**In a confined space, train the main stems
of a vigorous climbing rose in an S-shape.**

■ ABOVE
Correct pruning cuts. The clean cut, made
just above the bud, has been angled away
from it. Rain will run off, away from the
bud, rather than in to it, where the water
may collect and cause rotting.

■ ABOVE
Two incorrect pruning cuts. The stem on
the left has been cut too far away from the
emerging bud, while the one on the right
has been cut too close and the bud has
been damaged.

Pruning old roses

SPRING PRUNING FOR OLD ROSES

1 In early spring cut out all dead growth, going back to the base of the plant if necessary. At the same time, remove any crossing stems that rub against each other.

2 Cut back any other dead wood as far as live material.

3 Shorten laterals by between one-third and half their length if necessary. Cut back to a strong bud facing in the direction you want the stem to grow. Shorten any badly placed stems by one-third to a half.

Old roses generally flower on wood that is two years old or more. They need only very light pruning in early spring to tidy up their shape and to remove any dead or diseased stems that could cause problems later.

After spring pruning, apply a fertilizer to the rose. Water it well, and then mulch with well-rotted farmyard manure, bark chippings or garden compost. Feed the roses again after deadheading in the summer.

Old roses which are not performing well can sometimes be rescued by severe pruning. Cut back the oldest stems to ground level and others to within 15–30cm/6–12in of the ground. There will be plenty of strong growth in the following year, with flowers the year after that.

AN EASIER WAY TO PRUNE MODERN ROSES

Pruning a large rose bed, a rose hedge or a border of roses can seem a daunting and time-consuming task, and simply going over the rose bed with a powered hedge-trimmer (shears) is an appealing option. Traditionalist rose-growers will find the suggestion horrifying, but trials with the "rough and ready" method have shown that both large-flowered (hybrid tea) roses and cluster-flowered (floribunda) roses can actually produce better displays than when pruned conventionally. Established roses are surprisingly resilient and this crude method of pruning can be extremely successful.

There are some drawbacks, however. It is harder to monitor the roses individually, and they may become congested at the centre with a larger amount of dead wood. A congested rose bush, where air cannot circulate freely, traps moisture and thus increases the likelihood of fungi and diseases.

For a general garden display, however, using a powered hedge-trimmer is well worth considering, especially if you keep an eye open for dead or diseased shoots to prune out at the same time.

Although a powered hedge-trimmer will save time, you can use secateurs in the same way. Simply top the shoots at the required level.

Pruning shrub roses

In pruning terms, shrub roses include any species of wild rose and old-fashioned varieties of bushy roses that pre-date large-flowered and cluster-flowered varieties. Modern shrub roses, retaining many of the characteristics of the old-fashioned types, are pruned in the same way. They generally make much bigger bushes than large-flowered and cluster-flowered types, and they do not require such regular or intensive pruning. You can also use this technique to prune larger English roses. The main objective of pruning a shrub rose is to prevent it from becoming too large or congested.

1 Most species and early shrub roses will continue to flower well, even without pruning, but they become large and congested. Pruning will improve the overall appearance and help to keep the shrub compact. After some years there will be a lot of very old wood and probably congested stems.

2 On an old plant cut out one or two of the oldest or most congested shoots, taking them back to the base. Cut out any dead or diseased wood at the same time. The rose shown here naturally produces a lot of cane-like stems from the base; others will have fewer but thicker stems, more like those on a large-flowered rose.

3 Shorten the main shoots by between a quarter and a half. If the shoot is 1.2m/4ft tall, cut off 30–60cm/1–2ft. If the shrub has produced a lot of side shoots, shorten these by about two-thirds. Side shoots about 30cm/12in long should be cut back to about 10cm/4in.

4 Even when pruning has been done, you may be left with a substantial framework of stems. This is normal because a shrub rose usually makes a large bush. With those that shoot freely from the base, you can be more drastic.

5 Annual pruning will ensure that there is plenty of vigorous, young growth from the base of the plant. It encourages the production of plenty of flowers, even close to the ground.

Propagation

Propagating roses is extremely satisfying and it allows you to enjoy roses on a completely different level. Even if the new plants are not needed for your own garden, they make ideal gifts for friends.

Commercially, roses are propagated by grafting material from named varieties on to vigorous seedling rootstocks. This method is called budding. Rootstocks are not widely available outside the trade, although it may be possible to order them from some garden centres. Amateur gardeners usually choose to take hardwood or semi-ripe cuttings, or use the technique of layering.

When taking cuttings it is vital that you choose shoots that are free from diseases and pests and not too long between leaf joints (nodes). It's often best to take a cutting from the top of the plant, where it receives lots of light. Do not use any suckers that arise from the base of the plant: if the rose was grafted on to a different rootstock you may find you have propagated another plant entirely.

In general, only the most vigorous rose varieties will root readily and make good plants. But the only way to know for sure is to experiment, and propagation is often a matter of trial and error.

1 Prepare a trench 23–30cm/9–12in deep in the open ground and line it to one-third of its depth with sharp sand.

2 Cut well-ripened, pencil-thick stems from the rose, remove the soft tip and trim to a length of about 23cm/9in, with the base of the cut just below a leaf joint. Remove any leaves that remain on the stem.

3 Dip the base of the cutting in hormone rooting powder. Tap off any excess powder.

4 Insert the cutting in the trench, leaving about 7.5cm/3in above the soil surface. Firm in and water well.

Hardwood cuttings

Hardwood cuttings are taken in autumn, at the end of the growing season, when top growth has ceased and fully ripened. They can be rooted in the open ground as long as there is some protection from strong winds.

Check the cuttings periodically during the winter. If a hard frost causes the soil to erode and crack open, it may be necessary to re-firm the cuttings. In very cold areas, protect the cuttings with a cloche.

The cuttings should be rooted by the following autumn, when they can be transferred to their final position in the garden if they are sufficiently developed. Alternatively, they can be allowed to grow on for another year.

Many gardeners find hardwood cuttings the best method of propagation as the aftercare required is minimal.

LAYERING

1 Select a pliable shoot that can be brought down to ground level from near the base of the plant. Cut off all the leaves and side shoots from a section about 30cm/1ft long.

2 Around the point where the stem will touch the ground, work in peat or an alternative to make the soil more friable.

3 With a sharp knife, cut a tongue in the wood on the underside of the stem.

4 Keep the tongue open with a small piece of wood – a matchstick, for example – and dust the cut surfaces with hormone rooting powder.

5 Bring the stem down to the ground. To keep the wound just below soil level, fasten down the stem with a length of wire bent into a U shape.

6 Bend the shoot tip upwards and secure it to a cane inserted in the ground with lengths of wire or horticultural string tied in figures of eight.

Layering

A good method for roses that have long, flexible stems that can be brought down to ground level. Climbing roses are obvious candidates for layering, and ground-cover roses – descendants of the climbing species – can also be increased by this technique. You may even find that some roses layer themselves in favourable conditions.

Layering is a simple technique, and it can be a more reliable one than taking cuttings because the new plant remains attached to the parent while rooting. It is, however, usually feasible to produce only a few new rose plants by this method because only a small number of stems is likely to be suitable.

Roses are best layered in late summer. The layers should have rooted by the following spring, when they can be severed from the parent, and potted up or grown on in a nursery bed until large enough to be planted out in their final position. Some rose growers find it most convenient to layer directly into a pot of compost. The container is buried in the ground, and the plant is layered as usual. Once the rose has rooted, it can be severed from the parent plant, and the whole pot is then dug up.

Budding

Budding is a nurseryman's technique, widely practised within the trade as it allows saleable plants to be produced very quickly. Most amateur gardens prefer to take cuttings, which is a simpler but slower method of propagation. If you wish to increase your stock by budding you will need to acquire rootstocks, which are unfortunately not usually available to the public. The simplest method of accomplishing this is to contact a local commercial rose grower and ask if you can buy a rootstock. Patient gardeners can also raise their own stocks from seed.

Most roses are highly bred plants and have lost some of their vigour in the selection process. Budding is a technique that involves grafting buds from the parent plant (the scion) on to strongly growing rootstocks, usually of species roses such as *R. multiflora* or *R. canina*.

Budding is usually carried out from mid-summer onwards while the plants are still growing. You are more likely to be successful if you choose a wet day, when there is less chance of the propagating material drying out.

Select strong, healthy, well-ripened, non-flowering stems from the parent plant. To test for ripeness, bend one of the thorns. If the stem is ripe, the thorn will snap off cleanly. If the thorn is soft and flexible the stem is not yet ripe enough.

The knife you use should be sharp and clean. Ragged cuts will not heal properly and could provide an entry point for disease.

If the union between the plants is a success, new growth will begin from the scion the following spring. Leave to develop *in situ* for at least a year before transferring to its final position.

PROPAGATION BY BUDDING

1 Cut a strong, ripe, healthy stem from the parent plant.

2 Trim off the leaves and snap off the thorns cleanly.

3 Hold the stem so that the growing point is facing towards you. Place the blade of a knife behind a dormant bud. Carefully draw the knife towards you to cut beneath the bud. Pull the knife to tear off a tail of bark.

LAYERING

1 Select a pliable shoot that can be brought down to ground level from near the base of the plant. Cut off all the leaves and side shoots from a section about 30cm/1ft long.

2 Around the point where the stem will touch the ground, work in peat or an alternative to make the soil more friable.

3 With a sharp knife, cut a tongue in the wood on the underside of the stem.

4 Keep the tongue open with a small piece of wood – a matchstick, for example – and dust the cut surfaces with hormone rooting powder.

5 Bring the stem down to the ground. To keep the wound just below soil level, fasten down the stem with a length of wire bent into a U shape.

6 Bend the shoot tip upwards and secure it to a cane inserted in the ground with lengths of wire or horticultural string tied in figures of eight.

Layering

A good method for roses that have long, flexible stems that can be brought down to ground level. Climbing roses are obvious candidates for layering, and ground-cover roses – descendants of the climbing species – can also be increased by this technique. You may even find that some roses layer themselves in favourable conditions.

Layering is a simple technique, and it can be a more reliable one than taking cuttings because the new plant remains attached to the parent while rooting. It is, however, usually feasible to produce only a few new rose plants by this method because only a small number of stems is likely to be suitable.

Roses are best layered in late summer. The layers should have rooted by the following spring, when they can be severed from the parent, and potted up or grown on in a nursery bed until large enough to be planted out in their final position. Some rose growers find it most convenient to layer directly into a pot of compost. The container is buried in the ground, and the plant is layered as usual. Once the rose has rooted, it can be severed from the parent plant, and the whole pot is then dug up.

SEMI-RIPE CUTTINGS

1 Select a side shoot that is still green but beginning to turn woody at the base. Cut just above an outward-facing bud.

2 Trim the cutting at the base, just below a leaf joint.

3 Trim back the soft tip to leave a length of stem about 10cm/4in long.

4 Remove the lower leaves and all the thorns, if any. Dip the base of the cutting in hormone rooting powder and tap off the excess.

5 Using a dibber, insert the cuttings up to two-thirds of their length in the rooting medium.

6 Firm the cuttings with your fingers, then spray them with a solution of copper fungicide, which will both moisten the soil mix and kill off any fungal spores and bacteria.

Semi-ripe cuttings

In very cold areas you may have more success propagating roses using the method of semi-ripe cuttings. The cuttings from this technique need more attention, both while rooting and when overwintering. Given proper care, however, a higher proportion of plants are likely to root by this method than by taking hardwood cuttings.

7 Label the cuttings, then tent the pot with a plastic bag to prevent moisture loss. Support the bag with sticks or wire hoops to prevent contact between the plastic and the leaves, because moisture will accumulate at that point and attract bacteria. Keep the cuttings in a shady, frost-free place until rooted.

4 Pull off the pith behind the bud, using the knife if necessary.

5 Make a T-shaped cut in the rootstock, cutting no deeper than the bark. Ease back the bark with the tip of the knife.

6 Insert t... rootsto...

7 Trim back the tail so that it is level with the top of the T.

8 Bind the stem with a rubber tie and secure it with a pin. The rubber will stretch as the bud begins to swell and grow.

9 When t... the follo... Cut back the... and leave th...

■ BELOW
Roses such as this Portland rose 'Madame Knorr' are easy to propagate by taking semi-ripe cuttings.

■ ABOVE
After six to eight weeks the base of the cutting will callus over and new roots will begin to emerge.

Semi-ripe cuttings are taken from mid- to late summer as the current year's growth is beginning to ripen and become woody at the base but is still green and pliable. Root the cuttings in pots containing an inert mixture of peat and sharp sand. You need to check the cuttings periodically. Remove any fallen leaves that may rot and make sure the rooting medium stays fairly moist. Always water with a fungicidal solution to prevent disease.

Once the cuttings have rooted, usually by the following spring, they can be planted out and grown on in nursery beds, or potted up individually, using loam-based compost (soil mix).

Budding

Budding is a nurseryman's technique, widely practised within the trade as it allows saleable plants to be produced very quickly. Most amateur gardens prefer to take cuttings, which is a simpler but slower method of propagation. If you wish to increase your stock by budding you will need to acquire rootstocks, which are unfortunately not usually available to the public. The simplest method of accomplishing this is to contact a local commercial rose grower and ask if you can buy a rootstock. Patient

gardeners can also raise their own stocks from seed.

Most roses are highly bred plants and have lost some of their vigour in the selection process. Budding is a technique that involves grafting buds from the parent plant (the scion) on to strongly growing rootstocks, usually of species roses such as *R. multiflora* or *R. canina*.

Budding is usually carried out from mid-summer onwards while the plants are still growing. You are more likely to be successful if you choose a wet day, when there is less chance of the propagating material drying out.

PROPAGATION BY BUDDING

1 Cut a strong, ripe, healthy stem from the parent plant.

2 Trim off the leaves and snap off the thorns cleanly.

3 H po blade Carefu cut be off a t

Hybridization

The process by which new plant varieties are produced is called hybridization. It can occur in the wild, where two compatible species grow in close proximity, but the vast majority of garden hybrids arise as a result of deliberate crossing.

Hybridization is a sexual method of producing new plants. In common with the majority of flowering plants, roses have flowers with both male and female reproductive parts. To produce fertile seeds, pollen, borne on the stamens (male) from one flower, is brought into contact with the stigmas (female) of another. Seed develops in the ovary below the stigmas. Seedlings will share some characteristics with both parents, without being identical to either.

Rose breeders practise hybridization extensively. In any one year hundreds of crosses are made, but only a few of the resulting plants have commercial potential. To be commercially viable a new rose must be vigorous, hardy and disease-resistant, and have good colour and scent. It must also be of sufficient novelty to distinguish it from existing roses. One or more of these attributes may be absent if the rose scores highly in other categories. All new roses have to undergo extensive trials

1 Select the seed parent. Choose a flower that is not fully open and is unlikely to have been pollinated. Working from the outside, carefully pull off the petals.

2 Carefully remove the stamens with sterilized tweezers.

6 When it is fully open, pull all the petals to expose the reproductive parts.

7 Uncover the seed parent and brush the anthers of the pollen parent across the stigmas of the seed parent to transfer the pollen. Replace the bag and allow the hip to develop. Label the stem with the names of both parents.

before large-scale production can be considered. Given the fierce competition, it is unlikely that the amateur will raise a new rose with any significant future, but you can still produce good garden plants.

Since the rose as a genus has a vast gene pool and extensive interbreeding has already occurred, you can never be certain which characteristics will arise from any cross. Seedlings may bear no visible resemblance to either

of their parents. The pedigrees of many modern roses are given in *Modern Roses*, published by the American Rose Society, but beyond a certain point, the ancestry of all rose hybrids is a matter if conjecture.

Theoretically, all roses should cross with each other, but some varieties are so highly bred that they are sterile (mules) or partly so. Also, some varieties make better pollen parents than seed parents and vice

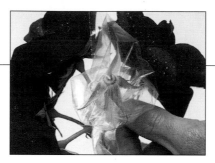

3 When you have removed the stamens you should be left with the bare exposed stigmas.

4 To prevent pollination from another source, cover the flower with a paper or plastic bag, secured with a wire tie.

5 Cut a flower that is not fully open from the pollen parent and keep it in water indoors.

8 Once the hip is ripe, cut it from the plant and slice it open to extract the seed. Mix the extracted seed with peat or an equivalent and grit or perlite in a plastic bag. Place it in the refrigerator for three or four weeks.

9 Sow the seed in trays or pots of seed compost and cover with grit.

10 Label the pots and place them in a cold frame to overwinter.

versa. In any breeding programme it is worth making the cross in both directions. When recording crosses, the convention is to cite the seed parent first. Thus, for example, label the seedlings 'Blue Moon' × 'Allgood' or 'Allgood' × 'Blue Moon'.

Rose seedlings can flower in their first year, although the blooms may not be typical. It will be a few years before you know whether you have produced an outstanding newcomer.

GENETIC ENGINEERING

Genetic engineering is a controversial technique by which specific genes (often from a different genus) are introduced into cells to ensure that a particular characteristic is inherited. Hitherto, its use has been largely confined to commercial, edible crop production, usually to promote disease resistance or a long shelf-life in foods.

There is every reason to suppose that in time, the techniques will be applied to ornamental plants, creating roses that, for instance, are particularly disease-resistant or hold their petals for a longer period. It should also be possible to extend the colour range to include the elusive blue. Genetic engineering requires laboratory conditions and is beyond the reach of the amateur gardener.

Pests, diseases and other disorders

Most roses are prone to a number of pests and diseases, but fortunately, most of these are easy to control. The incidence of disease and pest attack depends to some extent on climatic and regional variations – blackspot, for example, is more prevalent in some parts of the country than in others; mildew is more likely to be a problem if the weather is dry; and the aphid population will be affected by the winter survival of their predators.

As soon as the weather warms up, watch for signs of pest and disease infestation. Treat immediately, before population numbers have time to build up. Aphids can be particularly damaging, as they attack young shoot tips and cause subsequent distortion of growth.

In some seasons poor weather provides perfect conditions for the spread of fungal diseases, especially blackspot. An annual tar-oil winter wash applied to the stems and surrounding soil will reduce the reservoir of fungal spores and the need for extensive spraying with fungicide later on.

Some rose varieties are more susceptible to problems than others, but well-fed roses that are growing strongly can usually survive any attack, provided you act quickly. In addition, modern roses have a greatly improved disease-resistance.

Maintaining good standards of garden hygiene decreases the likelihood and the severity of any problems. Regularly clear up all plant debris, such as fallen leaves, both from the roses and also from other plants, as these may rot and harbour disease. You should also burn or otherwise dispose of any rose prunings for the same reason – do not put them on the compost heap. Make sure that the plants have enough space around them to ensure good air circulation. You may need to rethink your planting scheme if they become overcrowded as they develop.

Systemic insecticides and fungicides are applied as a spray and are absorbed by the plant. They do not kill the pest or disease directly, so their effect is not immediate. Repeated applications are usually necessary. Always follow the manufacturer's instructions.

The following are some of the problems which you are most likely to encounter. Most can be easily remedied if caught early.

■ RIGHT
Pre-empt problems by spraying against aphids in spring.

Aphids

The aphid that is most likely to attack roses is the greenfly, and these sap-sucking insects are usually spotted near the start of the season, clustering at the ends of stems and developing flower buds. They cause stunting and distortion of growth and may transmit viruses.

The aphids seen early in the year usually result from a failure to destroy prunings from the previous season that may harbour eggs. In practice, however, aphids are virtually endemic, and you are likely to encounter aphids every season.

To control aphids spray plants with a proprietary systemic insecticide as soon as you notice an infestation and repeat as directed by the manufacturer. A specific aphicide containing pirimicarb will leave beneficial insects such as ladybirds and lacewings unharmed.

Neatly notched leaves indicate the
activities of leaf-cutting bees.

Organic gardeners may remove
aphids by hand, spray with soft soap
or use an insecticide based on derris
or pyrethrum. Sometimes spraying
with plain water will disperse the
pest, but such treatment will have to
be repeated daily. Although
infestations may be severe, the pest is
easy to control, and long-term
damage can easily be avoided.

Leaf-cutting bee

Neat, semicircular or circular holes
are cut out from the leaf margins.
The bees use the portions of leaf to
make nests for their young. The
damage is largely cosmetic and will
not affect the health of established
plants. If the damage is severe, disturb
the insects with a fly swat, taking care
not to be stung. Bees are beneficial
pollinators and do not justify the use
of chemicals.

Leaf-rolling sawfly

In late spring or early summer rose
leaflets become tightly rolled around
freshly laid eggs. The caterpillar eats
the leaves as it emerges.

At the leaf-rolling stages, leaves
can be picked off if the infestation is
light. For more severe attacks, leave
the foliage in place and spray with a
systemic insecticide. You will not
reverse damage already caused, but
you will reduce the emerging
population that lays eggs in
subsequent years. If you have had the
problem one year, you can expect it
the next, although you can achieve
some protection by spraying the
undersides of the leaves with
insecticide in late spring or very early
summer before the adults lay eggs.

Balling

Flowers have a slack appearance, and
the petals turn brown and cling
together so that the flowers fail to
open properly. This may happen if
there is prolonged wet weather while
the buds are developing or if rain is
followed by hot sun. Aphid
infestation early in the season can
also lead to balling. Some roses are
more susceptible than others.

This disorder is impossible to
control. Balling is a seasonal
problem, which does not affect the
overall health of the plant, but you
should remove balled flowers that
may otherwise rot and allow diseases
to take hold. Balled flowers are
sometimes infected with fungi and
dieback may occur.

Roses with very delicate petals are
the most susceptible to balling, but
positioning them where they will
receive adequate sunlight and
ventilation to dry the blooms will
help to minimize the risk of rain
damage. Deadhead promptly, by
cutting back to a healthy bud or leaf.

■ LEFT
**Balling is caused by wet weather. It is not a
common problem, but some rose varieties
are prone to it.**

Calendar

Early spring

Improve the soil and plant new stock. On established plants, cut out any dead, diseased or damaged wood and shorten the remaining stems (ideally before the new leaves emerge, but after any danger of frost has passed). Fork fertilizer around the base of the roses as growth emerges, water in well and apply a 5–7.5cm/2–3in layer of mulch at the base of established plants. Cut back the rootstock on roses that were budded during the previous summer and that are showing signs of fresh growth. Renovate any old or neglected plants by pruning and feeding. Plant container-grown roses in the garden and also any bare-root roses that have not already been planted. In areas with very cold winters, prune repeat-flowering roses.

Mid- to late spring

Continue to plant new container-grown stock, remembering to keep them well watered until they are established. Check for and begin to control aphid infestations, leaf-rolling sawfly and blackspot. Remove any suckers. Apply a preventative fungicide as leaves emerge.

Mid-summer

Deadhead regularly and boost with rose fertilizer after the first flush of flowers. If necessary, prune after flowering. Increase your stock by taking semi-ripe cuttings (vigorous types only) or by budding. Keep a watch for suckers. Plant new stocks (container-grown roses only). In periods of prolonged hot, dry weather, water roses in open ground. Water roses in containers regularly and feed with liquid fertilizer. Continue to check for and control aphids, blackspot, rust and mildew. Visit garden centres and other gardens, read new specialist catalogues and begin to plan for autumn ordering, especially of roses that may be less readily available in local garden centres.

Old roses

Deadhead repeat-flowering roses and any others not grown for their decorative hips. Trim hedges after flowering unless grown for their hips. Thin twiggy growth on gallicas to improve air circulation.

Climbing roses

Shear over large ramblers. Tie in new shoots of climbers throughout the growing season. Layer ground-cover roses after flowering.

■ BELOW
In summer, tie in the shoots of climbers
while they are still young and flexible.

Late summer

Water plants regularly if the weather
is hot. Continue to take semi-ripe
cuttings of vigorous plants or layer
them if suitable.

Old roses

Peg down stems of hybrid perpetuals
and other types that produce long,
flexible stems. Tie in strong, new
shoots on roses trained as climbers.

Climbing roses

Tie in strong new shoots to extend
the framework.

Early autumn

Fork in bonemeal around the base of
the plants, water in well and mulch
with garden compost. Apply a high-
potash fertilizer to plants that are not
growing well. Rake up and burn
fallen rose leaves. Take hardwood
cuttings of vigorous roses. Place
orders with specialist nurseries.

Climbing roses

Prune to remove all the old,
unproductive wood, cutting back to
the base where necessary. Tie in
shoots securely to prevent damage
during winter gales.

Mid- to late autumn

In climates with a mild winter only,
begin pruning repeat-flowering roses.
Begin to dig over and improve soil
ready for new plantings. Begin
planting bare-root roses; the planting
season extends to early spring during
periods when the soil is not too wet,
dry or frozen.

Mid-winter

Browse through mail order catalogues
for any last-minute orders. Plant
bare-root or container-grown roses in
periods of good weather, when the
soil is not waterlogged, dry or frozen.
Apply a winter wash of tar oil if
wished to reduce the need for
fungicide sprays later in the season.

Late winter

In exposed sites, shorten the stems of
specimen roses to prevent wind-rock.
In frosty weather, if the soil surface
freezes and cracks, firm in hardwood
cuttings. In mild areas finish pruning
repeat-flowering roses. Improve the
soil for new spring plantings by
incorporating organic material. Plant
roses that were ordered earlier in the
winter or, if necessary, heel them in
until weather conditions improve.

Old roses

Tidy up hedges, such as *Rosa rugosa*,
that have ornamental hips and were
thus not pruned after flowering.

Plant early-flowering and late-flowering
rose varieties in the same bed to extend the
season of colourful displays from early
summer right through to late autumn.

Other Recommended Roses

*I*n addition to the roses illustrated in the individual catalogue sections, the following roses are also recommended. Synonyms and the date of introduction, where known, follow the name of the rose in parentheses. The dimensions of the rose under good growing conditions are given at the end of the description. The first figure indicates the rose's ultimate height, the second its spread.

■ RIGHT
The large, vivid yellow flowers of 'Freedom'
make this rose a good choice
for brightening up a garden.

Other recommended old roses

'Andersonii'

'Bloomfield Abundance'

'Agnes' (1922) Rugosa. Large, scented, double, pale yellow, occasionally buff, flowers appear in summer. A thorny rose.
1.8 × 1.2m/6 × 4ft.

'Andersonii' (uncertain) *Canina* hybrid. Lightly scented, single, deep pink flowers appear in mid-summer, followed by red hips in autumn.
2.1 × 2.4m/7 × 8ft.

'Blanche Double de Coubert' (1892) Rugosa. Sweetly scented, semi-double, white flowers open flat from pointed, pinkish buds from summer to autumn.
1.5 × 1.2m/5 × 4ft.

'Bloomfield Abundance' (1920) Polyantha. Delicate, lightly scented, double, pale soft-pink flowers open from buds with long, feathery calyces from summer to autumn.
1.8 × 1.5m/6 × 5ft.

'Blush Damask' (uncertain) Damask. Sweetly scented, fully double, deep lilac-pink flowers are produced in mid-summer.
1.2 × 1.2m/4 × 4ft.

'Camaïeux' (1830) Gallica. Fragrant, fully double, white flowers, striped and splashed with crimson, are produced in mid-summer.
1.2 × 1m/4 × 3ft.

'Celsiana' (before 1750) Damask. Strongly fragrant, semi-double, deep rose-pink flowers are borne in clusters in mid-summer.
1.5 × 1.2m/5 × 4ft.

× *centifolia* (uncertain) Centifolia. Strongly scented, fully double, soft-pink flowers are produced in mid-summer.
1.5 × 1.5m/5 × 5ft.

× *centifolia* **'Muscosa'** (common moss rose, syn. 'Old Pink Moss'; around 1696). Moss. Fragrant, fully double, clear-pink flowers are borne in mid-summer.
1.5 × 1.5m/5 × 5ft.

'Commandant Beaurepaire' (syn. 'Panachée d'Angers'; 1874) Bourbon. Fragrant, double, deep pink flowers, splashed and striped with purple, maroon and paler pink, appear in mid-summer and, more sporadically, in autumn.
1.8 × 1.5m/6 × 5ft.

'Comtesse du Caÿla' (1902) China. Fragrant, semi-double, copper-orange flowers, which fade to salmon-pink, are produced from summer to autumn.
1.5 × 1.5m/5 × 5ft.

'Cornelia' (1925) Hybrid musk. Sweetly scented, double flowers, carried from summer to autumn, fade from apricot-pink to creamy pink.
1.5 × 1.5m/5 × 5ft.

'De Meaux' (pompon rose; syn. *R.* × *centifolia* var. *pomponia*, 'Rose de Meaux'; 1789) Centifolia. Sweetly scented, fully double, soft-pink flowers appear in mid-summer.
1 × 1m/3 × 3ft.

'De Rescht' (uncertain) Damask Portland. Heavily scented, fully double, deep magenta-red flowers appear in mid-summer then intermittently until autumn.
1 × 1m/3 × 3ft.

ecae Species. Small, scented, single, cupped, brilliant yellow flowers are borne in late spring to early summer. Delicate mid-green foliage with reddish stems. A tender plant, benefiting from shelter.
1.5 × 1.2m/5 × 4ft.

'Empereur du Maroc' (1858) Hybrid perpetual. Intensely fragrant, fully double, quartered-rosette flowers of a rich red, almost purple, colour appear in mid-summer and again in autumn.
1.2 × 1m/4 × 3ft.

'Felicia' (1928) Hybrid musk. Sweetly scented, fully double, pale pink flowers are carried from summer to autumn. Abundant foliage is greyish-green.
1.5 × 2.1m/5 × 7ft.

'Ferdinand Pichard' (1921) Bourbon. Richly scented, loosely double, deep pink flowers, striped

'Blanche Double de Coubert'

'Fru Dagmar Hastrup'

with crimson and purple, appear from mid-summer to autumn.
1.2 × 1.2m/4 × 4ft.

foetida (Austrian briar, Austrian yellow rose) Species. Unpleasantly scented, single, bright yellow flowers are borne in early summer. 'Persiana' is a popular cultivar.
1.5 × 1.5m/5 × 5ft.

× *francofurtana* (syn. 'Empress Josephine'; early 19th century) Gallica. Lightly scented, loosely double, bright pink flowers, veined with deeper pink, are produced in mid-summer.
1.2 × 1.2m/4 × 4ft.

'Frau Karl Druschki' (syn. 'Reine des Neiges', 'Snow Queen'; 1901) Hybrid perpetual. Scentless, fully double, pure-white flowers emerge from pink-tinged buds in summer.
1.2 × 1.2m/4 × 4ft.

'Fru Dagmar Hastrup' (syn. 'Frau Dagmar Hartopp'; 1914) Rugosa. Scented, single, light pink flowers are borne in summer and autumn.
1 × 1.2m/3 × 4ft.

'Frühlingsmorgen' (syn. 'Spring Morning'; 1942) Pimpinellifolia hybrid. Lightly scented, single, pale pink to creamy white flowers are carried in late spring. A thorny rose with greyish-green foliage
1.8 × 1.5m/6 × 5ft.

'Général Kléber' (1856) Centifolia moss. Large, fragrant, fully double, soft-pink flowers with a silky sheen are borne in mid-summer.
1.5 × 1.5m/5 × 5ft.

'Georg Arends' (1910) Hybrid perpetual. Fragrant, fully double, soft-pink flowers appear from mid- to late summer. Nearly thornless.
1.8 × 1.8m/6 × 6ft.

'Gloire de France' (syn. 'Fanny Bias'; before 1819) Gallica. Very fragrant, fully double, pale mauve-pink flowers appear in mid-summer.
1 × 1m/3 × 3ft.

'Great Maiden's Blush' (syn. 'Cuisse de Nymphe', 'La Séduisante'; 15th century or earlier) Alba. Sweetly fragrant, rosette, double, soft-pink flowers appear in mid-summer or later.
1.5 × 1.5m/5 × 5ft or more.

jacksonii 'Max Graf' (syn. 'Max Graf'; 1919) Rugosa. Fragrant, single, deep pink flowers with golden stamens are produced throughout summer. 0.6 × 2.4m/2 × 8ft.

'Katharina Zeimet' (syn. 'White Baby Rambler') Polyantha. Sprays of many sweetly scented, small, double, cupped, white flowers are borne almost continuously from summer to autumn. 50 × 50cm/20 × 20in or more.

'Lady Hillingdon' (1910) Tea. Fragrant, semi-double, apricot-yellow flowers open from long, pointed, copper-orange buds from summer until autumn or later. 75 × 60cm/2½ × 2ft.

'Madame Knorr' (syn. 'Comte de Chambord'; 1860) Portland. Sweetly scented, fully double, deep pink flowers are produced in summer with a repeat flowering in autumn. 1.2 × 1.2m/4 × 4ft.

'Madame Pierre Oger' (1878) Bourbon. Sweetly scented, fully double, pale creamy pink flowers are produced from summer to autumn. Leaves are light green. A good pillar rose. 1.8 × 1.2m/6 × 4ft.

'Marchesa Boccella' (syn. 'Jacques Cartier'; 1866) Damask Portland. Strongly scented, fully double, clear-

'Madame Knorr'

pink flowers, paler at the edges, are borne in summer and again, but unreliably, in autumn. 1.2 × 1.2m/4 × 4ft.

'Mevrouw Nathalie Nypels' (syn. 'Nathalie Nypels'; 1919) Polyantha. Sweetly scented, semi-double, clear-pink flowers, fading to blush pink, are borne from summer to autumn. 60 × 60cm/2 × 2ft.

'Mousseline' (syn. 'Alfred de Dalmas'; 1855) Portland moss. Fragrant, semi-double, cupped soft blush-pink to creamy white flowers are produced in mid-summer. 1.2 × 1.2m/4 × 4ft.

moyesii (1903) Species. Virtually scentless, single, crimson flowers with yellow stamens appear from early to mid-summer, followed in autumn by flagon-shaped, brilliant scarlet hips. 2.4 × 1.5m/8 × 5ft.

'Mrs John Laing' (1887) Hybrid perpetual. Large, sweetly scented, fully double, clear-pink flowers are freely produced from summer to autumn. Light green foliage. 1 × 1m/3 × 3ft.

odorata 'Viridiflora' (green rose; syn. 'Viridiflora', *R. chinensis* 'Viridiflora', 'Lü E'; before 1833) China. Curious rather than beautiful, scentless, double, purple-tinged green "flowers" (in reality modified leaves) are produced from summer to autumn. 1 × 0.6m/3 × 2ft.

'Penelope' (1924) Hybrid musk. Large, sweetly scented, semi-double, pale creamy pink flowers are borne in clusters from summer to autumn. 1 × 1m/3 × 3ft.

'Petite de Hollande' (syn. 'Normandica', 'Petite Junon de Hollande', 'Pompon des Dames'; about 1800) Centifolia. Clusters of small, sweetly scented, double, pompon-like flowers, clear-pink with darker centres, are borne in summer. 1 × 1m/3 × 3ft.

pimpinellifolia 'Plena' Species. Double, cupped, creamy white flowers are borne early in summer, followed by blackish hips. Rather a thorny rose, but with abundant small dark green leaves. 1 × 1.2m/3 × 4ft.

moyesii

'Pink Grootendorst' (1923) Rugosa. Scentless, carnation-like, double, clear-pink flowers have fimbriated (fringed) edges and are produced from summer to autumn. 1.8 × 1.5m/6 × 5ft.

primula (incense rose; 1911) Species. Lightly scented, single, pale yellow flowers appear in late spring. The leaves are aromatic when wet. 1.8 × 1.8m/6 × 6ft.

'Reine des Violettes' (syn. 'Queen of the Violets'; 1860) Hybrid perpetual. Heavily scented, fully double, deep red flowers, ageing to dove-grey, are produced from summer to autumn. 1.8 × 1.8m/6 × 6ft.

'Reine Victoria' (syn. 'La Reine Victoria'; 1872) Bourbon. Sweetly scented, fully double, pink flowers are produced from summer to autumn. 1.8 × 1.2m/6 × 4ft.

rubiginosa (sweet briar, eglantine; syn. *R. eglanteria*) Species. Clusters of lightly scented, single, pink flowers are carried amid fragrant leaves in mid-summer, followed by scarlet hips. 2.4 × 2.4m/8 × 8ft.

'Saint Nicholas' (1950) Damask. Fragrant, semi-double, rich pink flowers with yellow stamens appear in mid-summer, followed by red hips in the autumn. Leaves are dark green and plentiful. 1.2 × 1.2m/4 × 4ft.

'Sarah van Fleet' (1926) Rugosa. Sweetly scented, light pink flowers open to reveal yellow stamens from summer to autumn. 1.8 × 1.2m/6 × 4ft or more.

'Sneezy' (uncertain) Polyantha. Masses of single, pink flowers are produced from summer to autumn. 30 × 30cm/12 × 12in.

'Souvenir du Docteur Jamain' (1865) Hybrid perpetual. Fragrant, fully double, wine-red flowers are carried in summer and autumn. 1.8 × 1.8m/6 × 6ft.

'Spong' (1805) Centifolia. Small, rounded, pompon-like, clear-pink flowers are carried amongst abundant foliage in mid-summer. 1.2 × 1m/4 × 3ft.

'The Bishop' (uncertain) Centifolia. Fragrant, fully double, cerise-purple

odorata 'Viridiflora'

flowers appear in mid-summer and then fade to lilac-mauve. 1.5 × 1m/5 × 3ft.

'Tour de Malakoff' (1856) Centifolia. Heavily scented, fully double, cupped, rich magenta-purple flowers, which age to dove-grey, are produced in mid-summer. 1.8 × 1.5m/6 × 5ft.

'Variegata di Bologna' (1909) Bourbon. Heavily scented, fully double, pale lilac-pink flowers, striped with intense crimson-purple, appear in mid-summer and autumn. Prone to blackspot. 1.8 × 1.8m/6 × 6ft.

'Yvonne Rabier' (1910) Polyantha. Lightly scented, double, creamy white flowers are borne from summer to autumn. Foliage is bright green and plentiful. 45 × 40cm/18 × 16in.

Other recommended modern roses

'**Abbeyfield Rose**' (syn. 'Cochrose'; 1985) Large-flowered or hybrid tea. Lightly scented, fully double, deep pink flowers are borne from summer to autumn. Good for bedding. 75 × 60cm/2½ × 2ft.

'**Allgold**' (1956) Cluster-flowered or floribunda. Scented, double, bright yellow flowers are produced throughout summer and autumn. 75 × 50cm/30 × 20in.

'**Anisley Dickson**' (syn. 'Dickimono', 'Dicky', 'Müncher Kindl'; 1983) Cluster-flowered or floribunda. Only lightly scented, double, salmon-pink flowers are produced from summer to autumn. Good in containers. 1 × 0.75m/3 × 2½ft.

'**Anna Livia**' (syn. 'Kormetter', 'Trier 2000'; 1985) Cluster-flowered or floribunda. Sprays of scented, double, clear-pink flowers are carried from summer to autumn. Suitable for a low hedge. 75 × 60cm/2½ × 2ft.

'**Anvil Sparks**' (syn. 'Ambossfunken') Large-flowered or hybrid tea. Shapely buds open to coral-red flowers striped and spotted with yellow. Healthy. 1 × 1m/3 × 3ft.

'**Bright Smile**' (syn. 'Dicdance'; 1980) Cluster-flowered or floribunda. Fragrant, semi-double, clear bright yellow flowers, which are rain-resistant, open flat from summer to autumn. Good disease resistance. 45 × 45cm/18 × 18in.

'**Carefree Beauty**' (syn. 'Bucbi'; 1977) Shrub. Fragrant, semi-double, creamy buff-pink flowers are carried on spreading stems all summer. 1.2 × 1.2m/4 × 4ft.

'**Champagne Cocktail**' (syn. 'Horflash'; 1985) Cluster-flowered or floribunda. Fragrant, double, light yellow flowers, suffused with pink, appear from summer to autumn. Good for bedding. 1 × 0.6m/3 × 2ft.

'**Chanelle**' (1959) Cluster-flowered or floribunda. Fragrant, semi-double to double, creamy buff-pink flowers are borne through summer and autumn. Good disease resistance. 75 × 60cm/ 2½ × 2ft.

'**City of Leeds**' (1966) Cluster-flowered or floribunda. Lightly scented, semi-double, salmon-pink flowers are produced from summer to autumn. Good for bedding. 75 × 60cm/2½ × 2ft.

'**City of London**' (syn. 'Harukfore'; 1988) Cluster-flowered or floribunda. Sweetly scented, semi-double to double, soft-pink flowers appear from summer to autumn. A good bedding rose or grow as a specimen plant. 2.4 × 1.2m/8 × 4ft.

'Deep Secret'

'**Congratulations**' (syn. 'Korlift', 'Sylvia'; 1978) Large-flowered or hybrid tea. Fragrant, fully double, neat, deep pink flowers are borne from summer to autumn. 1.2 × 1m/4 × 3ft or more.

'**Crimson Glory**' (1935) Large-flowered or hybrid tea. Fragrant, fully double, deep red flowers, good for cutting, appear all summer. 60 × 60cm/ 2 × 2ft.

'**Dawn Chorus**' (syn. 'Dicquasar'; 1993) Large-flowered or hybrid tea. Only lightly scented, double, orange flowers, with yellow petal reverses, are borne from summer to autumn. 75 × 60cm/2½ × 2ft.

'**Dearest**' (1960) Cluster-flowered or floribunda. Fragrant, double, clear-pink flowers are produced from summer to autumn. 60 × 60cm/2 × 2ft.

'**Deep Secret**' (syn. 'Mildred Scheel'; 1977) Large-flowered or hybrid tea. Fragrant, double, deep red flowers are borne from summer to autumn. Good for cutting.
1 × 0.75m/3 × 2½ft.

'**Disco Dancer**' (syn. 'Dicinfra'; 1984) Cluster-flowered or floribunda. Only lightly scented, semi-double, bright orange-red flowers are produced from summer to autumn. Glossy foliage. Good in containers or as a hedge.
75 × 60cm/2½ × 2ft.

'**Doris Tysterman**' (1975) Large-flowered or hybrid tea. Fragrant, fully double, coppery orange flowers appear from summer to autumn. Good for bedding.
1.2 × 0.75m/4 × 2½ft.

'**Ena Harkness**' (1946) Large-flowered or hybrid tea. Fragrant, fully double, deep red flowers are produced from early summer to autumn.
75 × 60cm/2½ × 2ft.

'**English Miss**' (1978) Cluster-flowered or floribunda. Fragrant, fully double, camellia-like, soft blush pink flowers appear from summer to autumn. Good in containers.
75 × 60cm/2½ × 2ft.

'**Ernest H. Morse**' (syn. 'E.H. Morse'; 1965) Large-flowered or hybrid tea. Very fragrant, double, red

'Doris Tysterman'

flowers, which darken with age, are borne freely from summer to autumn.
75 × 60cm/2½ × 2ft.

'**Evelyn Fison**' (syn. 'Macev', 'Irish Wonder'; 1962) Cluster-flowered or floribunda. Virtually scentless, double, brilliant red flowers are produced from summer to autumn. Glossy foliage. Good for bedding.
70 × 60cm/28 × 24in.

'**Fairyland**' (syn. 'Harlayalong') Polyantha. Sweetly scented, cupped, fully double, rosette-shaped, soft pink flowers are borne in trusses from summer to autumn. Glossy foliage.
0.6 × 1.2m/2 × 4ft.

'**Fellowship**' (syn. 'Harwelcome,' 'Livin' Easy'; 1992). Cluster-flowered or floribunda. Fragrant, double, cupped, warm orange flowers appear from summer to autumn.
75 × 60cm/2½ × 2ft.

'**Fragrant Delight**' (1978) Cluster-flowered or floribunda. Fragrant, double, orange-tinged, salmon-pink flowers are produced from summer to autumn. Reddish-green foliage.
1 × 0.75m/3 × 2½ft.

'**Fragrant Hour**' Large-flowered or hybrid tea. Shapely, fragrant, salmon-pink flowers are produced in summer-autumn. Good for cutting.
1 × 1m/3 × 3ft.

'**Freedom**' (syn. 'Dicjem'; 1984) Large-flowered or hybrid tea. Only lightly scented, double, vivid yellow flowers are produced from summer to autumn. Good for bedding. Glossy mid-green foliage.
75 × 60cm/2½ × 2ft.

'**Gertrude Jekyll**' (syn. 'Ausbord'; 1986) Shrub. Large, very fragrant, fully double, deep pink flowers are borne from summer to autumn. Greyish-green foliage.
1.5 × 1m/5 × 3ft.

'**Glenfiddich**' (1976) Cluster-flowered or floribunda. Fragrant, double, golden-yellow flowers appear from summer to autumn. Glossy foliage.
75 × 60cm/2½ × 2ft.

'**Golden Wings**' (1956) Shrub. Lightly scented, single, pale golden-yellow flowers are produced throughout summer. Spreading habit.
1 × 1.2m/3 × 4ft.

'Simba'

'**Harry Wheatcroft**' Large-flowered or hybrid tea. Fragrant red flowers, borne in summer-autumn, are striped with rich golden yellow.
1 × 1m/3ft × 3ft.

'**Heritage**' (syn. 'Ausblush'; 1984) Shrub. Strongly scented, fully double, apricot-pink flowers are produced from summer to autumn.
1.2 × 1.2m/4 × 4ft.

'**Iced Ginger**' (1971) Cluster-flowered or floribunda. Only lightly scented, double, coppery pink flowers are borne from summer to autumn. Good for cutting.
1 × 0.75m/3 × 2½ft.

'**Josephine Bruce**' (1952) Large-flowered or hybrid tea. Very fragrant, shapely, double, rich deep crimson flowers are produced from summer to autumn. Makes a good standard.
75 × 60cm/2½ × 2ft.

'**Keepsake**' (syn. 'Kormalda', 'Esmeralda'; 1980) Large-flowered or hybrid tea. Fragrant, rain-resistant, fully double, warm pink flowers are are borne from summer to autumn.
75 × 60cm/2½ × 2ft.

'**Lovely Lady**' (syn. 'Dicjubell', 'Dickson's Jubilee'; 1986) Large-flowered or hybrid tea. Fragrant, fully double, warm pink flowers appear from summer to autumn.
80 × 70cm/32 × 28in.

'**Lovers' Meeting**' (1980) Large-flowered or hybrid tea. Slightly fragrant, double, warm pinkish-orange flowers are produced from summer to autumn. Makes a good standard. Bronze-tinged foliage.
75 × 75cm/2½ × 2½ft.

'**Marguerite Hilling**' (syn. 'Pink Nevada'; 1959) Shrub. Lightly scented, semi-double, pale pink flowers appear in mid-summer and again, spasmodically, in autumn.
1.8 × 2.4m/6 × 8ft.

'**Matangi**' (syn. 'Macman'; 1974) Cluster-flowered or floribunda. Only lightly scented, double, brilliant vermilion flowers with white eyes and petal reverses are borne from summer to autumn. Glossy foliage.
80 × 60cm/32 × 24in.

'**Mischief**' (syn. 'Macmi'; 1961) Large-flowered or hybrid tea. Only lightly scented, double, deep salmon-pink flowers are borne from summer to autumn. Prone to rust.
1 × 0.6m/3 × 2ft.

'**National Trust**' (syn. 'Bad Nauheim'; 1970) Large-flowered or hybrid tea. Virtually scentless, fully double, vivid red flowers are produced from summer to autumn.
60 × 60cm/2 × 2ft.

'**Piccolo**' (syn. 'Piccola', 'Tanolokip'; 1984) Cluster-flowered or floribunda. Virtually scentless, double, vivid red flowers, which are rain-resistant, are produced from summer to autumn.
50 × 50cm/20 × 20in.

'**Pot o' Gold**' (syn. 'Dicdivine'; 1980) Large-flowered or hybrid tea. Dainty, fragrant, fully double, golden-yellow flowers are borne from summer to autumn. Makes a good standard.
75 × 60cm/2½ × 2ft.

'**Precious Platinum**' (syn. 'Opa Pötschke'; 1974) Large-flowered or hybrid tea. Only lightly scented, fully double, luminous red flowers are produced from summer to autumn.
1 × 0.6m/3 × 2ft.

'**Prima Ballerina**' (syn. 'Première Ballerina'; 1957) Large-flowered or hybrid tea. Sweetly scented, double, warm pink flowers are borne from summer to autumn. Leathery foliage.
1 × 0.6m/3 × 2ft.

'**Princess Michael of Kent**' (syn. 'Harlightly'; 1981) Cluster-flowered or floribunda. Sweetly scented, fully double, clear yellow flowers are produced from summer to autumn. Glossy foliage. Good in containers. 60 × 50cm/24 × 20in.

'**Remember Me**' (syn. 'Cocdestin'; 1984) Large-flowered or hybrid tea. Only lightly scented, fully double, warm coppery orange flowers are borne from summer to autumn. Glossy, dark green foliage. 1 × 0.6m/3 × 2ft.

'**Rose Gaujard**' (syn. 'Gaumo'; 1957) Large-flowered or hybrid tea. Fragrant, fully double, cherry red flowers with pale pink petal reverses are produced from summer to autumn. Good for cutting. 1 × 0.75m/ 3 × 2½ft.

'**Rosemary Harkness**' (syn. 'Harrowbond'; 1985) Large-flowered or hybrid tea. Fragrant, double, orange-yellow to salmon-pink flowers appear from summer to autumn. Glossy foliage. Good for cutting. 80 × 80cm/32 × 32in.

'**Royal Highness**' (syn. 'Königliche Hoheit'; 1962) Large-flowered or hybrid tea. Strongly fragrant, shapely, fully double, blush pink flowers are borne from summer to autumn. 1 × 0.6m/3 × 2ft.

'**Ruby Wedding**' Large-flowered or hybrid tea. Double, scented, deep velvety-red flowers are produced in succession throughout summer and autumn. Glossy leaves. 75 × 75cm/2½ × 2½ft.

'**Silver Jubilee**' (1978) Large-flowered or hybrid tea. Lightly scented, fully double, soft pink flowers shaded with apricot-pink are borne freely from summer to autumn. 1 × 0.75m/3 × 2½ft.

'**Simba**' (syn. 'Goldsmith', 'Helmut Schmidt', 'Korbelma'; 1981) Large-flowered or hybrid tea. Scented, double, clear yellow, rain-resistant flowers are produced from summer to autumn. Good for cutting. 75 × 60cm/2½ × 2ft.

'**Tango**' (syn. 'Macfirwal', 'Rock 'n' Roll', 'Stretch Johnson'; 1988) Cluster-flowered or floribunda.

'The Lady'

Lightly scented, semi-double flowers, the petals, fimbriated (frilled) at the edges, are orange-red with white rims, yellow at the base and on the reverse, and are borne in summer to autumn. Good for bedding. 75 × 60cm/2½ × 2ft.

'**Tequila Sunrise**' (syn. 'Dicobey', 'Beaulieu'; 1989) Large-flowered or hybrid tea. Only lightly scented, double, vivid yellow flowers with scarlet petal edges appear from summer to autumn. 75 × 60cm/2½ × 2ft.

'**The Lady**' (syn. 'Fryjingo'; 1985) Shrub. Fragrant, double, yellow flowers, flushed salmon-pink and rain-resistant, are produced from summer to autumn. 1 × 0.6m/3 × 2ft.

'**Valencia**' (syn. 'Koreklia'; 1989) Large-flowered or hybrid tea. Fragrant, double, warm golden-yellow flowers are carried from summer to autumn. Tolerates light shade. Leathery, glossy foliage. 1 × 0.6m/3 × 2ft.

'**Warm Wishes**' (syn. 'Fryxotic'; 1994) Large-flowered or hybrid tea. Sweetly scented, double, warm salmon-pink flowers are borne from summer to autumn. Glossy foliage. Good for cutting. 1 × 0.75m/3 × 2½ft.

Other recommended climbing roses

'**Alister Stella Gray**' (syn. 'Golden Rambler'; 1894) Climbing noisette. Clusters of very fragrant, fully double, quartered-rosette, deep yellow flowers are borne from summer to autumn. Vigorous upright stems with mid-green, glossy foliage. Suitable for growing into a tree.
5 × 3m/16½ × 10ft.

'**Altissimo**' (syn. 'Delmur'; 1966) Climber. Single, cupped, vivid red flowers, with golden stamens, are produced from summer to autumn. A stiffly upright plant.
3 × 2.4m/10 × 8ft.

'**Bad Neuenahr**' Climbing rose with large, double, clear red flowers borne in summer and autumn.
3 × 1.5m/10ft × 5ft.

'**Bantry Bay**' (1967) Climbing large-flowered or climbing hybrid tea. Large, freely borne clusters of lightly scented, cupped, semi-double, clear pink flowers open flat from summer to autumn. Glossy foliage.
4 × 2.4m/13 × 8ft.

'**Belle Portugaise**' (syn. 'Belle of Portugal') Climbing tea. Sweetly scented, pointed, double, salmon-pink flowers are carried in summer. Large, glossy leaves. A vigorous plant.
6 × 3m/20ft × 10ft.

'**Blush Rambler**' (1903) Rambler. Clusters of sweetly scented, cupped,

'Bantry Bay'

semi-double, pale pink flowers are borne in mid- to late summer. The glossy foliage is abundant and mid-green in colour. This rose is suitable for growing into a tree or over a pergola. It has a spreading habit.
4 × 5m/13 × 16½ft.

'**Céline Forestier**' (1842) Climbing noisette. Fragrant, rounded, double, quartered, creamy yellow flowers appear from late spring to autumn. Requires some protection in winter.
2.4 × 1.2m/8 × 4ft.

'**City Girl**' (syn. 'Harzorba'; 1994) Climber. Fragrant, semi-double, creamy pink flowers are carried from summer to autumn. Glossy, dark green foliage.
2.4 × 2.4m/8 × 8ft.

'**Climbing Etoile de Hollande**' (1931) Climbing large-flowered or climbing hybrid tea. Fragrant,

'Blush Rambler'

cupped, double, deep red flowers appear throughout summer.
6 × 5m/ 20 × 16½ft.

'**Climbing Lady Hillingdon**' (1917) Climbing tea. Sweetly scented, double, apricot-yellow flowers open from pointed buds from summer to autumn. Requires the protection of a west- or south-facing wall. Dark green foliage with reddish stems.
5 × 2.4m/16½ × 8ft.

'**Climbing Masquerade**' (1958) Climbing cluster-flowered or climbing floribunda. Clusters of semi-double flowers, which open yellow, then change to pink and age to red, are borne from summer to autumn, with all colours appearing on the plant simultaneously.
2.4 × 1.5m/8 × 5ft.

'**Climbing Mrs Sam McGredy**' (1937) Climbing large-flowered or

yellow flowers are produced from summer to autumn.
2.4 × 2.1m/8 × 7ft.

'**Niphetos**' Climbing tea rose. Round, double white flowers are borne in summer with a second, less abundant, flush in autumn. Light green, pointed leaves.
3 × 2m/10 × 6½ft.

'**Paul's Himalayan Musk**' (syn. 'Paul's Himalayan Rambler'; 'Paul's Himalayan Musk Rambler'; 1916) Rambler. Clusters of fragrant, double, rosette-shaped, pale pink flowers are borne in summer. A thorny rose.
10 × 10m/33 × 33ft.

'**Paul's Scarlet Climber**' (1916) Climber. Clusters of virtually scentless, cupped, double, bright red flowers, which gradually age to purplish-grey, are borne in summer. It will tolerate some shade.
3 × 3m/ 10 × 10ft.

'**Penny Lane**' (syn. 'Hardwell') Climbing rose with a succession of fragrant, honey-coloured flowers all summer.
4 × 1.8m/13 × 6ft

'**Ramona**' (syn. *R. × amenoides* 'Ramonda', 'Red Cherokee'; 1913) Climber. Virtually scentless, single, intense red flowers open flat to reveal golden stamens in early summer.
2.4 × 3m/8 × 10ft.

'**Ritter von B**[...]
Climber. Larg[...]
small, double[...]
produced in s[...]
3 × 1.5m/10 [...]

'**Rosy Mantle**[...]
Slightly fragra[...]
pink flowers [...]
to autumn. [...]
rather sparse. [...]
2.4 × 1.8m/8 [...]

'**Royal Gold**' [...]
flowered or cl[...]
Slightly fragra[...]
flowers are pr[...]
again in autu[...]
2.4 × 1.2m/8 [...]

'**Sander's Wh**[...]
Clusters of fr[...]
deep, rosette,[...]
produced in l[...]
3 × 2.4m/10 [...]

'**Sophie's Per**[...]
China') Clim[...]
of well-scent[...]
semi-double, [...]
overlaid with [...]
are borne cor[...]
to autumn. [...]
2.4 × 1.2m/8[...]

'**Souvenir de**[...]
(1920) Awar[...]
large-flowere[...]
tea. Fragrant[...]

climbing hybrid tea. Fragrant, fully double, coppery red flowers are borne in mid-summer and again, but sporadically, in autumn. A stiffly upright plant. Foliage is glossy and reddish-green in colour.
3 × 3m/10 × 10ft.

'**Climbing Shot Silk**' (1931) Climbing large-flowered or climbing hybrid tea. Heavily fragrant, fully double, urn-shaped to cupped flowers of pink overlaid with yellow and orange, are produced in summer. Glossy dark green foliage.
3 × 2.4m/10 × 8ft.

'**Copenhagen**' (1964) Climbing large-flowered or climbing hybrid tea. Fragrant, double, scarlet flowers are carried in summer and autumn.
3 × 1.5m/10 × 5ft.

'**Crimson Shower**' (1951) Rambler. Clusters of double, rosette-shaped, bright red flowers are produced from summer to autumn. Glossy foliage.
2.4 × 2.1m/8 × 7ft.

'**Dorothy Perkins**' (1901) Rambler. Clusters of scentless, double, bright pink flowers appear from late summer to autumn.
3 × 3m/10 × 10ft.

'**Don Juan**' Climbing rose with a succession of large, fragrant, deep red flowers throughout summer.
3 × 1.5m/10 × 5ft.

'Climbing Shot Silk'

'**Dreaming Spires**' (1973) Climber. Large, pleasantly scented, double, rounded, rich yellow flowers are produced from summer to autumn. Foliage is glossy and dark green. This rose has a stiffly upright habit.
3 × 2.1m/ 10 × 7ft.

'**Easlea's Golden Rambler**' (syn. 'Easlea's Golden'; 1932) Rambler. Clusters of fragrant, fully double, rounded, apricot-yellow flowers, marked with red, appear in summer.
6 × 5m/20 × 16½ft.

'**Emily Gray**' (1918) Rambler. Clusters of sweetly scented, double, rounded, buff-yellow flowers are borne from early summer. Glossy, almost evergreen foliage. Often prone to mildew.
5 × 3m/16½ × 10ft.

'**Excelsa**' (syn. 'Red Dorothy Perkins'; 1909) Rambler. Clusters of rosette-

shaped, double, red flowers are produced in summer. Glossy dark green foliage. Lax habit. A suitable rose for growing into a tree or up a pillar.
4 × 3m/13 × 10ft.

'**Félicité Perpétue**' (syn. 'Climbing Little White Pet', 'Félicité et Perpétue'; 1827) Rambler. Fragrant, fully double, rosette-shaped, light pink to ivory white flowers are produced in summer. Almost evergreen in favourable conditions. This rose will tolerate some shade.
5 × 4m/16½ × 13ft.

filipes '**Kiftsgate**' Climbing rose. Clusters of single, flat, creamy white flowers are borne in late summer. Abundant, light green, glossy foliage. A very vigorous rose which works well grown into a tree.
10 × 10m/30 × 30ft.

'Dreaming Spires'

'François Juranville' (1906) Rambler. Fragrant, fully double, rosette-shaped, pale salmon-pink flowers are produced in summer. There is abundant glossy foliage. Prone to mildew in a dry site, particularly when grown against a wall.
6 × 5m/20 × 16½ft.

'Galway Bay' (syn. 'Macba'; 1966) Climbing large-flowered or climbing hybrid tea. Large, double, rich pink flowers are borne from summer to autumn.
3 × 1.8m/10 × 6ft.

'Goldfinch' (1907) Rambler. Scented, double, rosette-shaped, deep yellow flowers, fading to pale cream, are produced in summer. Comparatively free of thorns with attractive light green foliage. Tolerates some shade.
2.4 × 1.8m/8 × 6ft.

'Guinée' (1938) Climbing large-flowered or climbing hybrid tea. Very fragrant, fully double, cupped, rich dark red flowers are borne in summer. Dark stems and foliage. Prone to mildew.
5 × 2.1m/ 16½ × 7ft.

'Hamburger Phönix' (1954) Rambler. Slightly fragrant, semi-double, deep red flowers open flat in summer and autumn.
3 × 1.5m/10 × 5ft.

'Excelsa

'High
Climbe
flowers
autumn
4 × 2.4

'Leapir
1986) (
climbin
scented
salmon
summe
3 × 1.8

'Leverk
Cluster
yellow
summe
green fo
3 × 2.1

'Meg' (
flowere
Cluster
double,

Index

Acknowledgments

The publishers would like to thank the following people for their help in the production of this book: Ann Hartley, Long Buckby, Northants; Cants of Colchester, Colchester; Cottesbrooke Hall Gardens, Cottesbrooke, Northants; Gandy's Roses Ltd, North Kilworth, Leics; Haddonstone Ltd, East Haddon, North Hants; J.F. Arbuthnott, Stone, Worcs; Janine Hurry, Long Buckby; Northants; Mattock's Roses, Nuneham Courtenay, Oxon; Mr and Mrs A. Keech, Long Buckby, Northants; Mr and Mrs A. Shepherd, Long Buckby, Northants; Mr and Mrs Smith, Nobottle, Northants; Ravensthorpe Nursery, Ravensthorpe, Northants; Rearsby Roses, Rearsby, Leics; RHS Garden, Wisley; Royal National Rose Society, St Albans, Herts; Shirley Allen, Long Buckby, Northants; The Hon. Simon and Mrs Howard, Castle Howard, York.

All pictures were taken by Peter Anderson with the exception of the following:

t=top, b=bottom, l=left, r=right, c=centre

6–7 Garden Picture Library/Steven Wooster; 8–9 Marie O'Hara; 30 Garden Picture Library/Brian Carter; 55 Peter McHoy; 58 Peter McHoy; 76b Andrew Mikolajski; 78b Andrew Mikolajski; 82–83 Marie O'Hara; 86–92t Marie O'Hara; 92b David Austin; 93–94 (tl and bl) Marie O'Hara; 94b David Austin; 95tr Andrew Mikolajski; 95 (tl and b) Marie O'Hara; 96 Andrew Mikolajski; 97t Andrew Mikolajski; 97b Marie O'Hara; 98–99 (tl and b) Marie O'Hara; 99tr David Austin; 100 Marie O'Hara; 101tl David Austin; 101 (tr and br) Marie O'Hara; 102b Andrew Mikolajski; 103–114b Marie O'Hara; 114t David Austin; 115 Marie O'Hara; 118–119 The Harpur Garden Picture Library (Fudler's Hall, Chelmsford); 121 Peter McHoy; 125l The Harpur Garden Picture Library; 125r Peter McHoy; 126l The Harpur Garden Picture Library (Design: Tessa Hobbs); 127 The Harpur Garden Picture Library (Stellenberg); 132r Andrew Mikolajski; 139 Andrew Mikolajski; 142tr Andrew Mikolajski; 154tr A–Z Botanical Collection; 147 (tl and bl) Andrew Mikolajski; 150–151 Garden Picture Library/Neil Holmes; 155 Harry Smith Collection; 157 Harry Smith Collection; 160bl John Freeman; 160tr Harry Smith Collection; 170t Andrew Mikolajski; 171tr Andrew Mikolajski; 186-187 Marie O'Hara; 196 Garden Picture Library/Eric Crichton; 197–198 Marie O'Hara; 209 Marie O'Hara; 217 Marie O'Hara; 222 Marie O'Hara; 223 (tl, tc, tr, bl) Marie O'Hara; 231b Marie O'Hara; 238–241 Marie O'Hara; 242l Peter McHoy; 243 Peter McHoy

Additional photography by Peter McHoy and John Freeman.